Langenscheidt

Universal-Phrasebook Spanish

Edited by the
Langenscheidt Editorial Staff

Langenscheidt

Berlin · Munich · Vienna · Zurich
London · Madrid · New York · Warsaw

Phonetic transcriptions: The Glanze Intersound System
Illustrations: Kirill Chudinskiy

ISBN 978-3-468-98988-9

Printed in Germany

11010

Where?	**¿Dóndé?** ¿dōn'de?
Here.	**Aquí.** äkē'.
There.	**Allí.** älyē'.
On/To the right.	**A la derecha.** ä lä dere'tshä.
On/To the left.	**A la izquierda.** ä lä ēskyer'dä.
Straight ahead/on.	**Todo recto.** tō'dō rek'tō.
Do you have …?	**¿Tiene …?** ¿tye'ne …?
I would like …	**Quisiera …** kēsye'rä …
How much does this cost?	**¿Cuánto cuesta?** ¿ko͞o·än'tō ko͞o·es'tä?
Could you please write that down for me?	**Por favor, escribamelo.** pōr fävōr', eskrē'bämelō.
Where is …?	**¿Dónde está …?** ¿dōn'de estä' …?
Where *is/are* there …?	**¿Dónde hay …?** ¿dōn'de ī …?
Today.	**Hoy.** oi.
Tomorrow.	**Mañana.** mänyä'nä.
I don't want to.	**No quiero.** nō kye'rō.
I can't.	**No puedo.** nō po͞o·e'dō.
Just a minute, please.	**¡Un momento, por favor!** ¡o͞on mōmen'tō, pōr fävōr'!
Leave me alone!	**¡Déjeme en paz!** ¡de'heme en päs!

Last name
Apellido
First name
Nombre
Home Address
Dirección en su país

Date of birth
Fecha de nacimiento
Vacation address
Dirección durante las vacaciones

No. of *ID/passport*
Número del *carnét de identidad/pasaporte*

In case of emergency, please contact:
En caso de urgencia, por favor, avisar a

Important information (allergies, medicines, blood type, etc.):
Datos importantes (alergias, medicamentos, grupo sanguíneo, etc.)

In case of loss of traveler's checks, contact:

In case of loss of credit card, contact:

CONTENTS

1 HUMAN RELATIONS

2 ACCOMMODATIONS

3 ON THE WAY

4 FOOD AND DRINK

5 SIGHTSEEING

6 SHOPPING

7 ENTERTAINMENT AND SPORTS

8 POST OFFICE, BANK, INTERNET

9 EMERGENCIES

10 TIME AND WEATHER

HOW TO FIND IT

This phrase book contains all of the most important expressions and words you'll need for your trip. They have been divided up according to situations and organised into 10 **chapters**. The page borders have been colored to help you find things even more quickly.

Each chapter consists of **example sentences** and **lists of words** together with complementary vocabulary. This will help you put together exactly the right sentence you need for any situation. The easy-to-understand **basic grammar section** will give you further support.

Of course you can just show the person you're talking to the Spanish translation of the sentence you wish to say. But the easily distinguished blue **phonetic alphabet** will enable you to speak your chosen phrase without any knowledge of Spanish whatsoever. In order to give you an indication of the proper intonation, we have inserted punctuation marks into the phonetic spellings.

For vital situations we have also included **sentences that go from Spanish to English**, so that a Spanish person may also be able to communicate with you.

In order to cover as many different situations as possible we offer **alternatives** with many sentences; these are written in italics and separated by a slash:

Will I see you *tomorrow/ this evening?*	**¿Quedamos para *mañana/ esta tarde?*** ¿kedä'mōs pä'rä *mänyä'nä/es'tä tär'de?*

You can separate the alternatives into individual sentences, asking either:

Will I see you tomorrow?	**¿Quedamos para mañana?** ¿kedä'mōs pä'rä mänyä'nä?

or:

Will I see you this evening?	**¿Quedamos para esta tarde?** ¿kedä'mōs pä'rä es'tä tär'de?

When we offer more than two possibilities there will be an elipsis at that point in the sentence; the possible **phrases to complete your sentence** will be listed underneath:

I would like ...	**Quisiera ...** kēsye'rä ...
a list of hotels.	**una lista de hoteles.** o͞o'nä lēs'tä de ōte'les.
a street map.	**un plano de la ciudad.** o͞on plä'nō de lä syo͞odäd'.
a map of the subway.	**un plano del metro.** o͞on plä'nō del me'trō.

You can then put them together as needed, for example:

I would like a street map.	**Quisiera un plano de la ciudad.** kēsye'rä o͞on plä'nō de lä syo͞odäd'.

Often you will also find **sentence completions in parentheses.** You can include these in your communication as you like.

How much is it (more or less)?	**¿Cuánto cuesta (aproximadamente)?** ¿'ko͞o·än'tō ko͞o·es'tä (äprōksēmädämen'te)?

In Spanish the form of the word used is sometimes dependent upon the gender of either the person speaking or the person addressed. In these cases we have indicated the different forms by the symbols ♂ (masculine) and ♀ (feminine):

Are you married?	**¿Está ♂ casado?/♀ casada?** ¿estä ♂ käsä'dō?/♀ käsä'dä?

You would ask a man **¿Está casado?**, a woman **¿Está casada?**

In Spanish, nouns and their qualifying adjectives belong to either the masculine or feminine gender, and the articles differ accordingly. To clarify this we have used the abbreviations ***m*** for masculine and ***f*** for feminine words in the vocabulary lists. We have included the feminine endings with the adjectives only when they are irregular. You will find the rules for the regular endings in the **basic grammar section** of this book.

HOW DO YOU PRONOUNCE IT?

All words and phrases are accompanied by simplified pronunciation. The sound symbols are the ones you are familiar with from your high-school or college dictionaries of the *English language*, but applied here to *foreign languages* – a unique feature of Langenscheidt's Universal Phrasebooks.

Symbol	Approximate Sound	Examples
	VOWELS	
ä	The *a* of *father.*	*casa* kä'sä
e	The *e* of *met* (but tending toward the *a* of *fate*).	*meses* me'ses
ē	The *e* of *he.*	*camino* kämē'nō *ir* ēr
ī	The *i* of *time.*	*hai* ī *mosaico* mōsī'kō
ō	The *o* of *nose* (but without the "upglide").	*como* kō'mō *norte* nōr'te
oi	The *oi* of *voice.*	*estoy* estoi'
o͞o	The *u* of *rule* (but without the "upglide").	*agudo* ägo͞o'dō
ou	The *ou* of *house.*	*causa* kou'sä

Symbol	Approximate Sound	Examples
	CONSONANTS	
b	A sound that has to be learned by listening (and which differs from country to country). Until you have learned this sound, use the *b* of *bed.* See also v, below.	*hablar* äblär' *beber* beber'
d	The *d* of *do.*	*rendir* rendēr'
f	The *f* of *far*	*efecto* efek'tō
g	The *g* of *go.*	*gato* gä'tō
h̲	A sound that has to be learned by listening. (This "guttural" sound resembles the *ch* of Scottish *loch* and of German *Bach.*) *Until you have learned this sound, use the* h *of* hot.	*Juan* ho͞o än' *gente* h̲en'te
k	The *k* of *key,* the *c* of *can.*	*cubo* ko͞o'bō
l	The *l* of *love* (not of fall). (See also the combination ly, below.)	*lado* lä'dō
m	The *m* of *me.*	*mesa* me'sä
n	The *n* of *no.* (See also the combination ny, below.)	*andar* ändär'

Symbol	Approximate Sound	Examples
ng	The *ng* of *sing*.	*banco* bäng'kō
p	The *p* of *pin*.	*poco* pō'kō
r	The *r* of *run*, but with a stronger "trill" in many words, especially words with *rr*.	*rico* rē'kō *grande* grän'de *perro* pe'rō
s	The *s* of *sun*. (See also z, below.)	*servir* servēr'
t	The *t* of *toy*.	tiempo tyem'pō
tsh	The *ch* of *much*.	muchacha mo͞otshä'tshä
v	A sound that is usually identical to the b, above. But the pronunciation varies greatly; and for the sake of simplicity the letter *v* is represented here by v.	*vida* vē'dä *huevo* o͞o·e'vō
y	The *y* of *year*. (See also the combinations ly and ny, below.)	*yo* yō *hielo* ye'lō
z	The *z* of *zeal*. (Note: Spanish *s* is pronounced z before *b, d, g, l, m, n,* and *r.)*	*mismo* mēz'mō *desde* dez'de

Note these frequent combinations:

ly	as in *caballo* käbä'lyō or *julio* h̲o͞o'lyō
ny	as in *año* ä'nyō or *junio* h̲o͞o'nyō
o͞o·e	as in *bueno* bo͞o·e'nō
o͞o·ä	as in *cuanto* ko͞o·än'tō
o͞o'ē	as in *muy* mo͞o'ē
o͞o·ō	as in *cuota* ko͞o·ō'tä
e'ē	as in *rey* re'ē
e·o͞o	as in *neumático* ne·o͞omä'tēkō
ä·ē	as in *caída* kä·ē'dä

Words of more than one syllable are given with a stress mark.

A raised dot separates two neighboring vowel symbols, and occasionally two consonant symbols: *ahora* ä·ō'ra, *sangría* säng·grē'a. This dot is merely a convenience to the eye; it does not indicate a break in pronunciation.

Human Relations

HI AND BYE!

Good morning.	**¡Buenos días!** ¡bo͞o·e'nōs dē'äs!
Good afternoon.	**¡Buenas tardes!** ¡bo͞o·e'näs tär'des!
Good *evening*/*night.*	**¡Buenas noches!** ¡bo͞o·e'näs nō'tshes!
Hello/*Hi.*	**¡Hola!** ¡ō'lä!

INFO Before lunch, greet people with **¡Buenos días!**, from after lunch until dark with **¡Buenas tardes!** and after dark (at around 8 or 9 p.m.) with **¡Buenas noches!** At any time of day you can say **Hola, ¿qué tal?** (Hello, how's everything?). Respond to this with **¡Bien, gracias!** (Fine, thanks). **Adiós,** in addition to meaning 'Goodbye,' can also be used as a greeting in passing.

May I join you?	**¿Me puedo sentar aquí?** ¿me po͞o·e'dō sentär' äkē'?
Sorry, that seat's taken.	**No, lo siento, está ocupado.** nō, lō syen'tō, estä' ōko͞opä'dō.
How are you?	**¿Cómo *está*/*estás*?** ¿kō'mō *estä'* / *estäs'*?
How's everything?	**¿Qué tal?** ¿ke täl?
I'm sorry, but I have to go now.	**Lo siento, pero me tengo que ir.** lō syen'tō, pe'rō me teng'gō ke ēr.
Good-bye/*Bye.*	**¡Adiós!** ¡ädyōs'!

See you *soon/ tomorrow.*	**¡Hasta *luego/mañana*!** ¡äs'tä *lo͞o·e'gō/mänyä'nä*!
It was nice meeting you.	**Me alegro mucho de *haberle/haberte* conocido.** me äle'grō mo͞o'tshō de *äber'le/äber'te* kōnōse'dō.
Thanks, it was a very nice *afternoon/day.*	**Gracias, ha sido *una tarde/un día* muy agradable.** grä'syäs, ä sē'dō *o͞o'nä tär'de/o͞on dē'ä* mo͞o'e ägrädä'ble.

! **¡Buen viaje!** ¡bo͞o·en' vyä'he! Have a good trip!

SMALL TALK ...

... *about yourself and others*

What's your name?	**¿Cómo *se llama/te llamas*?** ¿kō'mō *se lyä'mä/ te lyä'mäs*?
My name is ...	**Me llamo ...** me lyä'mō ...
Where are you from?	**¿De dónde *es usted/eres*?** ¿de dōn'de *es o͞oste'/ e'res*?
I'm from the U.S.	**Soy de los los Estados Unidos.** soi de lōs estä'dōs o͞one'dōs
Are you married?	**¿*Está/Estás* ♂ casado/♀ casada?** ¿*estä'/ estäs'* ♂ käsä'dō/♀ käsä'dä?

INFO **Novio/Novia** mean both boyfriend/girlfriend and fiancé/fiancée. A male friend is simply **un amigo**, and a female friend **una amiga**. Titles such as **licenciado** (graduate), **profesor** (professor, teacher) or **ingeniero** (engineer) are frequently used. **Don** and **Doña** (+ person's first name) are terms of respect reserved for older men and women.

Do you have any children?	**¿*Tiene/Tienes* hijos?** ¿*tye'ne/ tye'nes* e'hōs?
How old are they?	**¿Qué edad tienen?** ¿ke edäd' tye'nen?
Do you have any brothers or sisters?	**¿*Tiene/Tienes* hermanos?** ¿*'tye'ne/tye'nen* ermä'nōs?
I have *a sister/ a brother.*	**Tengo *una hermana/un hermano.*** teng'gō *ōō'nä ermä'nä/ōōn ermä'nō.*
How old are you?	**¿Cuántos años *tiene/tienes*?** ¿kōō·än'tōs ä'nyōs tye'ne/tye'nes?
I'm … years old.	**Tengo … años.** teng'gō … ä'nyōs.
What sort of work do you do?	**¿A qué *se dedica/te dedicas*?** ¿ ä ke *se dedē'kä/te dede'käs*?
I'm a(n) …	**Soy …** soi …
What are you studying?	**¿Qué *estudia/estudias*?** ¿ke *estōō'dyä/ estōō'dyäs*?

… about home and vacation

Is this your first time here?	**¿Es la primera vez que *está/estás* aquí?** ¿es lä prēme'rä ves ke *vye'ne/ vye'nes* äke'?
No, I've been here before.	**No, ya he estado aquí antes.** nō, yä e estä'dō äke' än'tes.
Have you been here long?	**¿*Lleva/Llevas* ya mucho tiempo aquí?** ¿*lye'vä/ lye'väs* yä mo͞o'tshō tyem'pō äke'?
For … *days/ weeks.*	**Hace … *días/semanas.*** ä'se … *de'äs/ semä'näs.*
How much longer are you staying?	**¿Hasta cuándo *se queda/te quedas*?** ¿äs'tä ko͞o·än'dō *se ke'dä/ te ke'däs*?
I'm leaving tomorrow.	**Me voy mañana.** me voi mänyä'nä.
Two more weeks.	**Dos semanas más.** dōs semä'näs mäs.
Do you like it here?	**¿*Le/Te* gusta este lugar?** ¿*le/ te* go͞os'tä es'te lo͞ogär'?
I like it very much.	**Me gusta mucho.** me go͞os'tä mo͞o'tshō.
Mexico is a very beautiful country.	**México es un país muy bonito.** me'h̲ēkō es o͞on pä·ēs' mo͞o'ē bōnē'tō.

Have you ever been to the States?	**¿*Ha estado/Has estado* alguna vez en los Estados Unidos?** *¿ä estä'dō/äs estä'dō* älgōō'nä ves en lōs estä'dōs ōōne'dōs?
You should visit me if you come to the States.	**Venga a visitarme cuando vaya a los Estados Unidos.** veng'gä ä vēsētär'me kōō·än'dō vä'yä ä lōs estä'dōs ōōnē'dōs.
I'd love to show you the city.	***Le/Te* enseño la ciudad.** *le/te* ense'nyō lä syōōdäd'.

SOCIALIZING

Would you like to…?

What are you doing tomorrow?	**¿Qué *va/vas* a hacer mañana?** ¿ke *vä/väs* ä äser' mänyä'nä?
Would you like to get together *tomorrow/this evening*?	**¿Quedamos para *mañana/esta tarde*?** ¿kedä'mōs pä'rä *mänyä'nä/es'tä tär'de*?
Yes, I'd love to.	**Sí, con mucho gusto.** sē, kōn mōō'tshō gōōs'tō.
I'm sorry, I already have plans.	**Lo siento, pero ya he quedado.** lō syen'tō, pe'rō yä e kedä'dō.
Would you like to join me for dinner this evening?	**¿Cenamos juntos esta noche?** ¿senä'mōs hōōn'tōs es'tä nō'tshe?

I'd like to invite you to dinner.	**Quisiera *invitarle/invitarte* a cenar.** kēsye'rä *ēnvētär'le/ēnvētär'te.*

See also: Dining with Friends (p. 117), Going out in the Evening (p.191)

1

When/Where should we meet?	**¿*Cuándo/Dónde* nos encontramos?** ¿*ko͞o·än'dō/dōn'de* nōs enkōnträ'mōs?
Let's meet at … o'clock.	**Vamos a encontrarnos a las …** vä'mōs ä enkōnträr'nōs ä läs…
I'll pick you up at … o'clock.	***Le/Te* paso a buscar ⟨Sp: recoger⟩ a las …** *le/te* pä'sō ä bo͞oskär' ⟨Sp: rekōh̲er'⟩ ä läs…
May I take you home?	**¿Puedo acompañarle a casa?** ¿po͞o·e'dō äkōmpänyär'le ä kä'sä?
May I see you again?	**¿Nos vemos otra vez?** ¿nōs ve'mōs ō'trä ves?

No, thanks.

Sorry, I already have plans.	**Lo siento, ya he quedado.** lō syen'tō, yä e ke'dä'dō.
I'm waiting for someone.	**Estoy esperando a alguien.** estoi' esperän'dō ä äl'gyen.
Leave me alone!	**¡Déjeme en paz!** ¡de'h̲eme en päs!
Go away!	**¡Váyase ya!** ¡väy'äse yä!

COMMUNICATING

Does anyone here speak English? **¿Hay alguien aquí que hable inglés?** ¿ī äl'gyen äke' ke ä'ble ēng·gles'?

? **¿Habla usted español?** ¿äb'lä o͞oste' espänyōl'? Do you speak Spanish?

Only a little. **Sólo un poco.** sō'lō o͞on pō'kō.

Please speak a little slower. **Por favor, hable un poco más despacio.** pōr fävōr', ä'ble o͞on pō'kō mäs despä'syō.

? **¿Entiende?** ¿entyen'de? Do you understand?

Yes, I understand. **Si, entiendo.** sē, entyen'dō.

Sorry, I don't understand. **Lo siento, no entiendo.** lō syen'tō, nō entyen'dō.

Please repeat that. **¿Puede repetir, por favor?** ¿po͞o·e'de repetēr', pōr fävōr'?

What is this called in Spanish? **¿Cómo se dice esto en español?** ¿kō'mō se dē'se es'tō en espänyōl'?

What does . . . mean? **¿Qué significa ...?** ¿ke sēgnēfē'kä ...?

WHAT DO YOU THINK?

1

It *was*/*is* very nice here.	**Me *ha gustado*/*gusta* mucho este lugar.** me *ä go͞ostä'dō/go͞os'tä* mo͞o'tshō es'te lo͞ogär.
Very well!	**¡Muy bien!** ¡mo͞o'ē byen'!
Great!	**¡Estupendo!** ¡esto͞open'dō!
I like it.	**Me gusta.** me go͞os'tä.
With pleasure.	**Con mucho gusto.** kōn mo͞o'tshō go͞os'tō.
OK.	**De acuerdo. ⟨Sp: Vale.⟩** de äko͞o·er'dō. ⟨Sp: vä'le.⟩
It's all the same to me.	**Me da igual.** me dä ēgo͞o·äl'.
I don't know yet.	**No lo sé todavía.** nō lō se tōdävē'ä.
Maybe.	**Quizás.** kēsäs'.
Too bad!	**¡Qué pena!** ¡ke pe'nä!
Unfortunately that won't be possible.	**Lo siento, pero no es posible.** lō syen'tō, pe'rō nō es pōsē'ble.
I'd prefer …	**Preferiría …** preferērē'ä …
I don't like it.	**No me gusta.** nō me go͞os'tä.
No.	**No.** nō.
Absolutely not.	**¡De ninguna manera!** ¡de nengoo'nä mane'ra!

BASIC PHRASES

Please; Thank You

Could you please help me?	**¿Podría usted ayudarme?** ¿pōdrē'ä o͞oste' äyo͞odär'me?
Yes, of course.	**Sí, con mucho gusto.** sē, kōn mo͞o'tshō go͞os'tō.

INFO If you want to attract someone's attention to ask them something you can say **¡Perdón!**, or **¡Oiga, por favor!**

No, thank you.	**No, gracias.** nō, grä'syäs.
Thank you.	**Gracias.** grä'syäs.
Thank you very much.	**Muchas gracias.** mo͞o'tshäs grä'syäs.
Thank you, that's very nice of you.	**Muy amable de su parte, gracias.** mo͞o'e ämä'ble pōr so͞o pär'te, grä'syäs.
You're welcome.	**De nada.** de nä'dä.

Sorry!

Excuse me! (*apology*)	**¡Perdóneme!** ¡perdōn'eme!
I'm sorry.	**Lo siento.** lō syen'tō.
It was a misunderstanding.	**Ha sido un malentendido.** ä sē'dō o͞on mälentendē'dō.

Best wishes!

Congratulations. **¡Felicitaciones!** ¡felēsētäsyō'nes!

Have a good trip! **¡Buen viaje!** ¡bo͞o·en' vyä'h̲e!

Enjoy *yourself/ yourselves*! **¡Que se *divierta/diviertan*!** ¡ke se *dēvyer'tä/dēvyer'tän*!

Good luck! **¡Buena suerte!** ¡bo͞o·en'ä so͞o·er'te!

Merry Christmas! **¡Feliz Navidad!** ¡felēs' nävēdäd'!

Happy New Year! **¡Próspero Año Nuevo!** ¡prōs'perō ä'nyō no͞o·e'vō!

1

Human Relations

address **la dirección** lä dēreksyōn'
to arrange to meet (someone) **quedar (con uno)** kedär'
arrive **llegar** lyegär'
boyfriend **el novio** el nō'vyō
brother **el hermano** el ermä'nō
child **el niño** el nē'nyō
city **la ciudad** lä syo͞odäd'
to come from **ser de** ser de
country **el país** el pä·ēs'
daughter **la hija** lä ē'h̲ä
father **el papá** ⟨**Sp: el padre**⟩ el päpä' ⟨Sp: el pä'dre⟩
friend *(male)* **el amigo** el ämē'gō
friend *(female)* **la amiga** lä ämē'gä

to get to know	**conocer** kōnōser'
girlfriend	**la novia** lä nō'vyä
to be glad	**alegrarse** älegrär'se
to go dancing	**ir a bailar** er ä bīlär'
to go out to eat	**ir a comer** er ä kōmer'
to have plans	**pensar hacer** pensär' äser'
husband	**el marido** el märē'dō
to invite (someone) to dinner	**invitar (a alguien) a cenar** ēnvētär' (ä äl'gyen) ä senär'
job	**la profesión** lä prōfesyōn'
to leave	**salir** sälēr'
to like *(I would like to)*	**querer** kerer'
to like *(it appeals to me)*	**gustar** go͞ostär'
to make a date	**citarse** sētär'se
married	**casado** käsä'dō
mother	**la mamá** ⟨**Sp: la madre**⟩ lä mämä' ⟨Sp: lä mä'dre⟩
no	**no** nō
please	**por favor** pōr fävōr'
to return	**volver** vōlver'
school	**la escuela** la esko͞o·e'lä
sister	**la hermana** lä ermä'nä
son	**el hijo** el ē'h̲ō
to speak	**hablar** ä'blär
student	**el estudiante** el esto͞odyän'te
to be called	**llamarse** lyämär'se
to understand	**entender** entender'

vacation	**las vacaciones *f/pl*** läs väkäsyō'nes
to wait	**esperar** esperär'
wife	**la esposa** lä espō'sä
to write down	**escribir** eskrēvēr'
yes	**sí** sē

1

FOR THE HANDICAPPED

I'm hard of hearing.	**No oigo bien.** nō oi'gō byen.
Can you speak a little louder?	**¿Podría hablar más alto?** ¿pōdrē'ä äblär' mäs äl'tō?
I'm physically handicapped.	**Soy minusválido.** soi mēno͞osvä'lēdō.
I can't walk very well.	**Tengo problemas para caminar.** teng'gō prōble'mäs pä'rä kämēnär'.
Can you please help me?	**¿Puede ayudarme, por favor?** ¿po͞o·e'de äyo͞odär'me, pōr fävōr'?
Do you have a wheelchair for me?	**¿Tiene usted una silla de ruedas para mí?** ¿tye'ne o͞oste' o͞o'nä sē'lyä de ro͞o·e'däs pä'rä mē?
Can you please take my luggage to the *room/taxi*?	**¿Puede llevarme el equipaje *al cuarto* 〈*Sp: a la habitación*〉/ *al taxi*?** ¿po͞o·e'de lyevär'me el ekēpä'h̲e *äl ko͞o·är'tō 〈Sp: ä lä äbētäsyōn'〉/ äl tä'ksē*?
Where is the elevator?	**¿Dónde está el ascensor?** ¿dōn'de estä' el äsensōr'?

Could you please dial for me? — **¿Podría usted marcarme el número?** ¿pōdrē'ä o͞oste' märkär'me el no͞o'merō?

Is it suitable for wheelchairs? — **¿Es apto para personas con silla de ruedas?** ¿es äp'tō pä'rä persō'näs kōn sē'lyä de ro͞o·e'däs?

Is there a ramp for wheelchairs? — **¿Hay una rampa para silla de ruedas?** ¿ī o͞o'nä räm'pä pä'rä sē'lyä de ro͞o·e'däs?

Where is the restroom for the handicapped? — **¿Dónde están los baños ⟨Sp: los servicios⟩ para minusválidos?** ¿'dōn'de estän' lōs bä'nyōs ⟨Sp: lōs servē'syōs⟩ pä'rä mēno͞osvä'lēdōs?

I need someone to accompany me. — **Necesito a alguien que me acompañe.** nesesē'tō ä äl'gyen ke me äkōmpä'nye.

BUSINESS CONTACTS

On the Phone

See also: Communicating (p. 24)

This is … from … — **Soy …, de la empresa …** soi …, de lä empre'sä …

I would like to speak to … — **Quisiera hablar con …** kēsye'rä äblär' kōn …

! **Le pongo.** le pōng'gō. — I'll connect you.

! **… está hablando.** … estä' äblän'dō. — … is busy at the moment.

! **… hoy no está aquí.** … oi nō estä' äkē'. — … is not here today.

1

? **¿Quiere dejar algún recado?** ¿kye're dehär' älgōōn' rekä'dō? — Would you like to leave a message?

May I leave a message for …? — **¿Puedo dejar un recado para …?** ¿pōō·e'dō dehär' ōōn rekä'dō pä'rä …?

At the Reception Desk

I'd like to see … — **Quisiera hablar con …** kēsye'rä äblär' kōn …

My name is … — **Me llamo …** me lyä'mō …

I have an appointment at … o'clock with … — **Tengo una cita a las … con …** teng'gō ōō'nä sē'tä ä läs … kōn …

! **Un momento, por favor.** ōōn mōmen'tō, pōr fävōr'. — One moment, please.

! **… ahora mismo viene.** … ä·ō'rä mēz'mō vye'ne. — … will be right here.

! **… está todavía en una reunión.** … estä' tōdävē'ä en ōō'nä re·ōōnyōn'. — … is still in a meeting.

! **Venga conmigo, le acompaño a …** veng'gä kōnmē'gō, le äkōmpä'nyō ä … — Please follow me. I'll show you to …

? **¿Podría esperar un momento, por favor?** ¿pōdrē'ä esperär' o͞on mōmen'tō, pōr fävōr'? — Would you please wait here a moment?

At Trade Fairs

I'm looking for the … booth.	**Estoy buscando el stand de la empresa …** estoi' bo͞oskän'dō el estän' de lä empre'sä …
Do you have any information on …?	**¿Tiene información sobre …?** ¿tye'ne ēnfōrmäsyōn' sō'bre …?
Do you also have pamphlets in English?	**¿Tiene también folletos en inglés?** ¿tye'ne tämbyen' fōlye'tōs en ēng·gles'?
Who can I ask?	**¿A quién me tengo que dirigir?** ¿ä kyen me teng'gō ke dērēh̲ēr'?

Business Contacts

address	**la dirección** lä dēreksyōn'
to advise	**avisar** ävēsär'
appointment	**la cita** lä sē'tä
booth	**el stand** el estän'
brochure	**el folleto** el fōlye'tō
building	**el edificio** el edēfē'syō
business contact *(person)*	**el interlocutor** el ēnterlōko͞otōr'
catalog	**el catálogo** el kätä'lōgō
conference	**la conferencia** lä kōnferen'syä
consortium	**el consorcio** el kōnsōr'syō

copy	**la copia** lä kō'pyä
customer	**el cliente** el klē·en'te
department	**el departamento** el depärtämen'tō
department head	**el jefe de departamento** el h̲e'fe de depärtämen'tō
documents	**los documentos** ***m/pl*** lōs dōko͞omentōs
fax machine	**el telefax** el teleräks'
felt-tip pen	**el rotulador para transparencias** el rōto͞olädōr' pä'rä tränspären'syäs
information	**la información** lä ēnfōrmäsyōn'
informations booth	**el stand de información** el estän' de ēnfōrmäsyōn'
interpreter	**el intérprete** el ēnter'prete
management	**la gerencia** lä h̲eren'syä
manager	**el gerente** el h̲eren'te
marketing	**la distribución** lä dēstrēbo͞osyōn'
to meet	**encontrar** enkōnträr'
meeting	**la reunión** lä re·o͞onyōn'
meeting room	**la sala de reuniones** lä sä'lä de re·o͞onyō'nes
message	**el recado** el rekä'dō
microphone	**el micrófono** el mēkrō'fōnō
office	**la oficina** lä ōfēsē'nä
pavilion	**el pabellón** el päbelyōn'
to phone	**llamar por teléfono** lyämär' pōr tele'fōnō
price	**el precio** el pre'syō
price list	**la lista de precios** lä lēs'tä de pre'syōs

1

printer	**la impresora** lä ēmpre'sōrä
reception desk	**la recepción** lä resepsyōn'
representative	**el representante** el representän'te
secretary	**la secretaria** lä sekretär'yä
secretary's office	**la secretaría** lä sekretärē'ä
telephone	**el teléfono** el tele'fōnō
to notify	**informar** ēnfōrmär'
video	**el vídeo** el vē'de·ō
waiting room	**la sala de espera** lä sä'lä de espe'rä

Accommodations

INFORMATION

Where can I rent a room?	**¿Dónde se puede rentar ⟨Sp: alquilar⟩ un cuarto ⟨Sp: una habitación⟩?** ¿dōn'de se po͞o·e'de rentär' ⟨Sp: älkēlär'⟩ o͞on ko͞oär'tō ⟨Sp: o͞o'nä äbētäsyōn'⟩?
Could you recommend ...	**¿Puede usted recomendarme ...** ¿po͞o·e'de o͞oste' rekōmendär'me ...
a good hotel?	**un buen hotel?** o͞on bo͞o·en' ōtel'?
a reasonably-priced hotel?	**un hotel económico?** o͞on ōtel' ekōnō'mēkō?
a guest house?	**una casa de huéspedes?** o͞o'nä kä'sä de o͞o·es'pedes?
a room in a private home?	**un alojamiento en una casa particular?** o͞on älōh̲ämyen'tō en o͞o'nä kä'sä pärtēko͞olär'?
I'm looking for somewhere to stay ...	**Busco un alojamiento ...** bo͞os'kō o͞on älōh̲ämyen'tō ...
in a *central/quiet* location.	***céntrico / tranquilo.*** *sen'trēkō / träng·kē'lō.*
at the beach./ by the river.	***en la playa / cerca del río.*** *en lä plä'yä / ser'kä del rē'ō.*
What are the rates (approximately)?	**¿Cuánto cuesta (aproximadamente)?** ¿ko͞o·än'tō ko͞o·es'tä (äprōksēmädämen'te)?
Can you make a reservation for me there?	**¿Puede hacerme allí una reserva?** ¿po͞o·e'de äser'me älyē' o͞o'nä reser'vä?

Is there *a youth hostel/ a camping ground* here?	**¿Hay por aquí cerca *un albergue juvenil/un cámping*?** ¿ī pōr äkē' ser'kä *ōōn älber'ge hōōvenēl'/ōōn käm'pēng*?
Is it far from here?	**¿Está lejos de aquí?** ¿estä' le'hōs de äkē'?
How do I get there?	**¿Cómo llego allí?** ¿kō'mō lye'gō älyē'?
Can you draw me a map?	**¿Puede dibujarme el camino?** ¿pōō·e'de debōōhär'me el kämē'nō?

2

INFO There are hotel and motel accommodations in all price ranges in most Latin American cities. Only first class hotels have bathrooms; most economical hotels just have sinks in the rooms. In small towns with few accommodations you might consider an inn, **posada**, or a guest house, **casa de huéspedes**. There are also trailer parks, **parque de traylers**, and organized campgrounds in popular tourist destinations, especially along the coast.

HOTEL AND VACATION RENTAL

Hotel

I have a reservation.	**Tengo un cuarto reservado ⟨Sp: una habitación reservada⟩ aquí.** teng'gō ōōn kōō·är'tō reservä'dō ⟨Sp: ōō'nä äbētäsyōn' reservä'dä⟩ äkē'.
My name is…	**Me llamo …** me lyä'mō…

Here is my confirmation (number).	**Aquí tiene mi confirmación.** äkē' tye'ne mē kōnfērmäsyōn'.
Do you have a *double/single* room available	**¿Tienen un cuarto *doble/individual* libre ...?** ¿tye'nen o͞on ko͞o·är'tō *dō'ble/ēndēvēdo͞o·äl'* lē'bre ...?
for *one night/...nights*?	**para *un día/... días*?** pä'rä *o͞on dē'ä/... dē'äs*?
with bath	**con baño completo?** kōn bä'nyō kōmple'tō?
with shower	**con ducha ⟨Mex: regadera⟩?** kōn do͞o'tshä ⟨Mex: regäde'rä⟩?
with toilet	**con excusado ⟨Sp: wáter⟩?** kōn eskōosä'dō ⟨Sp: o͞o·ä'ter⟩?
with a view of the ocean?	**con vista al mar?** kōn vēs'tä äl mär?
with a balcony?	**con balcón?** kōn bälkōn'?
with air conditioning?	**con aire acondicionado?** kōn ä·ē're äkōndēsyōnä'dō?
I'd like a room *with a double bed/with twin beds.*	**Quisiera un cuarto *con cama matrimonial/con dos camas.*** kēsye'rä o͞on ko͞o·är'tō *kōn kä'mä mätrēmōnēäl'/kōn dōs kä'mäs.*

! **Lo siento, está todo ocupado.** lō syen'tō, estä' tō'dō ōko͞opä'dō. — Unfortunately we are fully booked.

! ***Mañana/El día* ... se quedará un cuarto libre.** *mänyä'nä/el dē'ä* ... se kedärä' o͞on ko͞o·är'tō lē'bre. — *Tomorrow/On the* ... there will be a room available.

What is the rate ...	**¿Cuánto cuesta ...?** ¿ko͞o·än'tō ko͞o·es'tä ...
with/withhout breakfast?	***con/sin* desayuno?** *kōn/sēn* desäyo͞o'nō?
with half board/ with full room and board?	**con *media pensión/pensión completa*?** kōn *me'dyä pensyōn'/ pensyōn' kōmple'tä*?
Is there a discount for children?	**¿Hacen descuento a los niños?** ¿ä'sen desko͞o·en'tō ä lōs nē'nyōs?
May I have a look at the room?	**¿Puedo ver el cuarto?** ¿po͞o·e'dō ver el ko͞o·är·tō?
Do you have anything ...	**¿No tienen algo ...** ¿nō tye'nen äl'gō ...
cheaper?	**más barato?** mäs bärä'tō?
larger?	**más grande?** mäs grän'de?
quieter?	**más tranquilo?** mäs träng·kē'lō?
It's very nice. I'll take it.	**Me gusta mucho. Me quedo con ello.** me go͞os'tä mo͞o'tshō, me ke'dō kōn e'lyō.
Can you set up a crib in the room?	**¿Puede poner una cama de niño?** ¿po͞o·e'de pōner' o͞o'nä kä'mä de nē'nyō?

? **¿Tiene equipaje?**
¿tye'ne ekēpä'he?

Do you have any luggage?

2

Can you have my luggage brought to the room?	**¿Podría llevarme el equipaje al cuarto?** ¿pōdrē'ä lyevär'me el ekēpä'he äl kōō·är'tō?
Where is the shower?	**¿Dónde está la ducha ⟨Mex: la regadera⟩?** ¿dōn'de estä' lä dōō'tshä ⟨Mex: lä regäde'rä⟩?
Where can I park my car?	**¿Dónde puedo dejar el carro ⟨Sp: el coche⟩?** ¿dōn'de pōō·e'dō dehär' el kä'rō ⟨Sp: el kō'tshe⟩?
Where is the dining *room/breakfast* room?	**¿Dónde está *el comedor/la sala de desayuno*?** ¿dōn'de estä' *el kōmedōr'/lä sä'lä de desäyōō'nō*?
Can I give you my valuables for safe-keeping?	**¿Puedo depositar los objetos de valor?** ¿pōō·e'dō depōsētär' lōs ōbhe'tōs de välōr'?
I'd like to pick up my valuables.	**Quiero recoger mis objetos de valor.** kye'rō rekōher' mēs ōbhe'tōs de välōr'.
Can you exchange money for me?	**¿Me podría cambiar dinero?** ¿me pōdrē'ä kämbyär' dēne'rō?
I'd like the key for room number …	**Por favor, la llave del número …** pōr fävōr', lä lyä've del nōō'merō …
Can I make a call to the States from my room?	**¿Se puede llamar por teléfono a los Estados Unidos desde mi cuarto?** ¿sē pōō·e'de lyämär' pōr tele'fōnō ä lōs estä'dōs ōōnē'dōs dez'de mē kōōär'tō?

Is there any mail/Are there any messages for me?	**¿Hay *correo/algún mensaje* para mí?** *¿ī kōre'ō/älgōōn' mensä'he* pä'rä mē?
I'd like a wakeup call tomorrow at… o'clock, please.	**Por favor, despiérteme mañana a las…** pōr fävōr', despyer'teme mänyä'nä ä läs…
We're leaving tomorrow.	**Mañana salimos.** mänyä'nä salē'mōs.
Would you please prepare my bill?	**Prepáreme la cuenta, por favor.** prepä'räme lä kōō·en'tä, pōr fävōr'.
I enjoyed being here.	**Me ha gustado mucho estar aquí.** me ä gōōstä'dō mōō'tshō estär' äkē'.
May I leave my luggage here until … o'clock?	**¿Puedo dejar mi equipaje aquí hasta las …?** ¿pōō·e'dō dehär' mē ekēpä'he äkē' äs'tä läs…?
Would you call a taxi for me, please?	**Por favor, llame un taxi.** pōr fävōr', lyä'me ōōn tä'ksē.

Vacation Rental

We have rented an apartment.	**Hemos rentado un apartamento.** e'mōs rentä'dō ōōn äpärtämen'tō.
Where can we pick up the keys?	**¿Dónde podemos recoger las llaves?** ¿dōn'de pōde'mōs rekōher' läs lyä'ves?

2

Where is the *fusebox*/*meter*?	**¿Dónde está** ***la caja de los fusibles*****/** ***el contador de la luz*****?** ¿dōn'de estä' *lä kä'hä de lōs fōōsē'bles/el kōntädōr' de lä lōōs*?
Could you please explain how the ... works?	**¿Podría explicarnos cómo funciona ...?** ¿pōdrē'ä eksplēkär'nōs kō'mō fōōnsyō'nä ...?
stove	**la estufa ⟨Sp: la cocina⟩?** lä estōō'fä ⟨Sp: lä kōsē'nä⟩?
dishwasher	**el lavavajillas?** el läväväh̲ē'lyäs?
washing machine	**la lavadora?** lä lävädō'rä?
Can you please tell us where there's ...?	**Por favor, díganos dónde hay ...** pōr fävōr', dē'gänōs dōn'de ī ...
a bakery?	**una panadería.** ōō'nä pänäderē'ä.
a grocery store?	**una tienda (de comestibles).** ōō'nä tyen'dä (de kōmestē'bles).
a market?/*a supermarket*?	***un mercado*****/** ***un supermercado*****.** *ōōn merkä'dō*/*ōōn sōōpermerkä'dō*.
a butcher's shop?	**una carnicería.** ōō'nä kärnēserē'ä.
Where do I put the trash?	**¿Dónde se deja la basura?** ¿dōn'de se de'h̲ä lä bäsōō'rä?
Where can I make a phone call?	**¿Dónde se puede llamar por teléfono?** ¿dōn'de se pōō·e'de lyämär' pōr tele'fōnō?

Where can I park my car?	**¿Dónde puedo dejar el carro ⟨Sp: el coche⟩?** ¿dōn'de pōō·e'dō dehär' el kä'rō ⟨Sp: el kō'tshe⟩?
Where's the nearest bus stop?	**¿Dónde está la parada del bus ⟨Mex: del camión, Sp: del autobús⟩ más próxima?** ¿dōn'de estä' lä pärä'dä del bōōs ⟨Mex: del kämyōn', Sp: del outōbōōs'⟩ mäs prō'ksēmä?

Complaints

Could I please have …	**¿Podría darme …** ¿pōdrē'ä där'me …
another blanket?	**otra cobija ⟨Sp: manta⟩?** ōt'rä kōbē'hä ⟨Sp: män'tä⟩?
another towel?	**otra toalla?** ōt'rä tō·ä'lyä?
a few more clothes hangers?	**unas perchas?** ōō'näs per'tshäs?
The window doesn't *open/close.*	**La ventana no se puede *abrir/cerrar.*** lä ventä'nä nō se pōō·e'de *äbrēr'/serär'.*
… doesn't work.	**… no funciona.** … nō fōōnsyō'nä.
The shower	**La ducha ⟨Mex: La regadera⟩** lä dōō'tshä ⟨Mex: lä regäde'rä⟩
The air conditioning	**El aire acondicionado** el ä·ē're äkōndēsyōnä'dō
The light	**La luz** lä lōōs

The toilet doesn't flush. **El excusado no funciona.**
el ekskōōsä'dō nō fōōnsyō'nä.

There is no (hot) water. **No hay agua (caliente).**
nō ī ä'gōō·ä (kälyen'te).

The faucet drips. **La llave ⟨Sp: el grifo⟩ gotea.**
lä lyä've ⟨Sp: el grē'fō⟩ gōte'ä.

The drain / The toilet is stopped up. ***El desagüe / El excusado* está tapado ⟨Sp: atascado⟩.** *el desä'gōō·e / el ōō·ä'ter* estä' täpä'dō ⟨Sp: ätäskä'dō⟩.

Hotel and Vacation Rental

adapter	**el adaptador** el ädäptädōr'
additional week	**la semana adicional** lä semä'nä ädēsyōnäl'
apartment	**el apartamento** el äpärtämen'tō
balcony	**el balcón** el bälkōn'
bath(room)	**el baño** el bä'nyō
bed	**la cama** lä kä'mä
bed linens	**la ropa de cama** lä rō'pä de kä'mä
bill	**la cuenta** lä kōō·en'tä
blanket	**la cobija ⟨Sp: la manta⟩** la kōbē'h̲ä ⟨Sp: lä män'tä⟩
breakfast	**el desayuno** el desäyōō'nō
breakfast buffet	**el buffet de desayuno** el bōōfe' de desäyōō'nō
breakfast room	**la sala de desayuno** lä sä'lä de desäyōō'nō
broken	**roto** rō'tō

bungalow	**el bungalow** el bo͞ong'gälō
chair	**la silla** lä sē'lyä
to clean	**limpiar** lēmpyär'
closet	**el armario** el ärmär'yō
cold water	**el agua fría** el ä'go͞o·ä frē'ä
complaint	**el reclamo** 〈**Sp: la reclamación**〉 el reklä'mō 〈Sp: lä reklämäsyōn'〉
complete cleaning	**la limpieza general** lä lēmpye'sä h̲enеräl'
crib	**la cama de niño** lä kä'mä de nē'nyō
cup	**la taza** lä tä'sä
cutlery	**los cubiertos** lōs ko͞obyer'tōs
dining room	**el comedor** el kōmedōr'
dinner	**la cena** lä se'nä
dirty	**sucio** so͞o'syō
door	**la puerta** lä po͞o·er'tä
double room	**el cuarto** 〈**Sp: la habitación**〉 **doble** el ko͞o·är'tō 〈Sp: lä äbētäsyōn'〉 dō'ble
extra charges	**los gastos adicionales** ***m/pl*** lōs gäs'tōs ädēsyōnä'les
fan	**el ventilador** el ventēlädōr'
first floor	**el primer piso** 〈**Sp: la planta baja**〉 el prēmer' pē'sō 〈Sp: lä plän'tä bä'h̲ä〉
floor	**el piso** el pē'sō
full room and board	**la pensión completa** lä pensyōn' kōmple'tä
gas bottle	**la bombona** lä bōmbō'nä
glass *(drinking)*	**el vaso** el vä'sō
high season	**la temporada alta** lä tempōrä'dä äl'tä

hot water **el agua caliente** el ä'go͞o·ä kälyen'te
hotel **el hotel** el ōtel'
key **la llave** lä lyä've
lamp **la lámpara** lä läm'pärä
light **la luz** lä lo͞os
light bulb **el bombillo ⟨Mex: el foco, Sp: la bombilla⟩** el bōmbē'lyō ⟨Mex: el fō'kō, Sp: lä bōmbē'lyä⟩
lock **la cerradura** lä serädo͞o'rä
low season **la temporada baja** lä tempōrä'dä bä'h̲ä
luggage **el equipaje** el ekēpä'h̲e
lunch **el almuerzo** el älmo͞o·er'sō
maid **la camarera ⟨Arg, Chi: la mucama⟩** lä kämäre'rä ⟨Arg, Chi: lä mo͞okä'mä⟩
mattress **el colchón** el kōltshōn'
mosquito net **el mosquitero** el mōskēte'rō
outlet **el enchufe** el entsho͞o'fe
patio **la terraza** lä terä'sä
plate **el plato** el plä'tō
plug **la clavija de enchufe** lä klävē'h̲ä de entsho͞o'fe
pool **Mex: la alberca ⟨Arg, Par: la pileta, Sp: la piscina⟩** Mex: lä älber'kä ⟨Arg, Par: lä pēle'tä, Sp: lä pēsē'nä⟩
pre-season **la temporada baja** lä tempōrä'dä bä'h̲ä
rate **la tasa** lä tä'sä
reception desk **la recepción** lä resepsyōn'

refrigerator	**el refrigerador ⟨Arg, Par: la heladera, Sp: el frigorífico⟩** el refrēh̲erädōr' ⟨Arg, Par: lä eläde'rä, Sp: el frēgōrē'fēkō⟩
registration	**la inscripción** lä ēnskrēpsyōn'
rent *(noun)*	**el arriendo ⟨Sp: el alquiler⟩** el äryen'dō ⟨Sp: el älkēler'⟩
to rent	**rentar ⟨Sp: alquilar⟩** rentär' ⟨Sp: älkēlär'⟩
to reserve	**reservar** reservär'
reserved	**reservado** reservä'dō
room	**el cuarto ⟨Sp: la habitación⟩** el ko͞o·är'tō ⟨Sp: lä äbētäsyōn'⟩
room with half board	**la media pensión** lä me'dyä pensyōn'
safe	**la caja fuerte** lä kä'h̲ä fo͞o·er'te
shower	**la ducha ⟨Mex: la regadera⟩** lä do͞o'tshä ⟨Mex: lä regäde'rä⟩
single room	**el cuarto ⟨Sp: la habitación⟩ individual** el ko͞o·är'tō ⟨Sp: lä äbētä-syōn'⟩ ēndēvēdo͞o·äl'
sink	**el lavatorio ⟨Sp: el lavabo⟩** el lävätōr'yō ⟨Sp: el lävä'bō⟩
stairs	**la escalera** lä eskäle'rä
table	**la mesa** lä me'sä
table service	**la vajilla** lä väh̲ē'lyä
telephone	**el teléfono** el tele'fōnō
toilet	**el baño ⟨Mex: el excusado, Sp: el wáter,** *in restaurant etc:* **los servicios⟩** el bä'nyō ⟨Mex: el eksko͞osä'dō, Sp: el o͞o·ä'ter, lōs servē'syōs⟩

toilet paper	**el papel higiénico** el päpel' ēhē·e'nēkō
towel	**la toalla** lä tō·ä'lyä
trash	**la basura** lä bäsōō'rä
trash can	**el cubo de la basura** el kōō'bō de lä bäsōō'rä
vacation apartment rental	**el apartamento ⟨Sp: el piso⟩ para las vacaciones** el äpärtämen'tō ⟨Sp: el pē'sō⟩ pä'rä läs väkäsyō'nes
vacation home rental	**la casa para las vacaciones** lä kä'sä pä'rä läs väkäsyō'nes
water	**el agua** el ä'gōō·ä
water faucet	**la llave ⟨Arg, Per: el caño, Sp: el grifo⟩** lä lyä've ⟨Arg, Per: el kä'nyō, Sp: el grē'fō⟩
to work	**funcionar** fōōnsyōnär'

YOUTH HOSTEL, CAMPING

Youth Hostel

Is anything available?	**¿Les queda algo libre?** ¿les ke'dä äl'gō lē'bre?
I'd like to stay for ...nights.	**Quiero quedarme ... noches.** kye'rō kedär'me ... nō'tshes.
How much is it per night (per person)?	**¿Cuánto cuesta por noche (por persona)?** ¿kōōän'tō kōō·es'tä pōr nō'tshe (pōr persō'nä)?

Do you have a double room?	**¿Tienen también un cuarto ⟨Sp: una habitación⟩ doble?** ¿tye'nen tämbyen' o͞on ko͞o·är'tō ⟨Sp: o͞o'nä äbētäsyōn'⟩ dō'ble?
Is breakfast included?	**¿Está incluído el desayuno?** ¿estä' ēnklo͞o·ē'dō el desäyo͞o'nō?
How much is	**¿Cuánto cuesta ...** ¿ko͞o·än'tō ko͞o·es'tä...?
breakfast?	**el desayuno?** el desäyo͞o'nō?
lunch?	**la comida?** lä kōmē'dä?
dinner?	**la cena?** lä se'nä?
Where can I get something to *eat/drink*?	**¿Dónde puedo comprar algo para *comer/beber*?** ¿dōn'de po͞o·e'dō kōmprär' äl'gō pä'rä *kōmer'/beber'*?
Where is the dining room?	**¿Dónde está el comedor?** ¿dōn'de estä' el kōmedōr'?
Can I rent bed linen here?	**¿Se puede alquilar ropa de cama?** ¿se po͞o·e'de älkēlär' rō'pä de kä'mä?
Where are the rest rooms?	**¿Dónde están los baños ⟨Sp: servicios⟩?** ¿dōn'de estän' los bä'nyōs ⟨Sp: servē'syōs⟩?
Could I wash clothes here?	**¿Se puede lavar la ropa aquí?** ¿se po͞o·e'de lävär' lä rō'pä äkē'?
Do you have lockers?	**¿Tienen consigna?** ¿tye'nen kōnsēg'nä?

2

When do you lock the doors?
¿Hasta qué hora se puede entrar por la noche? ¿äs'tä ke ō'rä se pōō·e'de enträr' pōr lä nō'tshe?

What's the best way to get to the city center?
¿Cuál es la mejor forma para ir al centro de la ciudad? ¿kōō·äl' es lä mehōr' fōr'mä pä'rä ēr äl sen'trō de lä syōōdäd'?

Where's the nearest bus stop?
¿Dónde está la parada de bus ⟨Mex: camión, Sp: autobús⟩ más próxima? ¿dōn'de estä' lä pärä'dä de bōōs ⟨Mex: kämyōn', Sp: outōbōōs'⟩ mäs prō'ksēmä?

Camping

May we camp on your property?
¿Está permitido acampar en su terreno? ¿estä' permētē'dō äkämpär' en sōō tere'nō?

INFO In Latin America and in Spain you should camp only on official campsites.

Do you still have room for…?
¿Les queda todavía algún sitio libre para …? ¿les ke'dä tōdävē'ä älgōōn' sē'tyō lē'bre pä'rä…?

What is the charge for…
¿Cuánto hay que pagar por… ¿kōō·än'tō ī ke pägär' pōr…

…adults and… children?
… adultos y … niños? … ädōōl'tōs ē … nē'nyōs?

a car with camper?	**un carro ⟨Sp: coche⟩ con caravana?** o͞on kä'rō ⟨Sp: kō'tshe⟩ kōn käräva'nä?
a motor home?	**una casa rodante ⟨Sp: un coche-vivienda⟩?** o͞ona kä'sä rōdän'te ⟨Sp: o͞on kō'tshē vēvyen'dä⟩?
a tent?	**una carpa ⟨Sp: tienda de campaña⟩?** o͞o'nä kär'pä ⟨Sp: tyen'dä de kämpä'nyä⟩?
Do you also rent *cabins/campers*?	**¿Se alquilan también *bungalows/caravanas*?** se älkē'län tämbyen' *bo͞ong'gälōs/käräva'näs*?
We'd like to stay *one night/…nights.*	**Queremos quedarnos *un día/… días.*** kere'mōs kedär'nōs *o͞on dē'ä/… dē'äs.*
Where are the wash-rooms?	**¿Dónde están los lavabos?** ¿dōn'de estän' lōs lävä'bōs?
Where can I…	**¿Dónde puedo …** ¿dōn'de po͞o·e'dō …
flush out the camper waste water?	**vaciar el sanitario?** väsyär' el sänētär'yō?
fill up with fresh water?	**llenar con agua limpia?** lyenär' kōn ä'go͞o ä lēm'pyä?
dump waste water?	**vaciar el agua de fregar?** väsyär' el ä'go͞o·ä de fregär'?
Do you have power hookups here?	**¿Hay aquí una toma de corriente?** ¿ī äkē' o͞o'nä tō'mä de kōryen'te?

Is there a grocery store here?	**¿Hay aquí una tienda de comestibles ⟨Mex: de abarrotes⟩?** ¿ī äkē' o͞o'nä tyen'dä de kōmestē'bles ⟨Mex: de äbä'rrōtes⟩?
Can I *rent/exchange* gas bottles?	**¿Se pueden *alquilar/cambiar* aquí bombonas?** ¿se po͞o·e'den *älkēlär'/kämbyär'* äkē' bōmbō'näs?
May I borrow a(n) ..., please?	**Por favor, ¿puede prestarme ...?** pōr fävōr', ¿po͞o·e'de prestär'me ...?

Youth Hostel and Camping

air mattress	**el colchón hinchable ⟨Sp: la colchoneta⟩** el kōltshōn' ēntshä'ble ⟨Sp: la cōltshōne'tä⟩
bed linens	**la ropa de cama** lä rō'pä de kä'mä
bedroom	**el dormitorio ⟨Mex: la recámara⟩** el dōrmētōr'yō ⟨Mex: lä rekä'märä⟩
breakfast	**el desayuno** el desäyo͞o'nō
to camp	**acampar** äkämpär'
camper (vehicle)	**la caravana** lä kärävä'nä
camping	**el campamento ⟨Sp: el cámping⟩** el kämpämen'tō ⟨Sp: el käm'pēng⟩
camping permit	**la tarjeta de cámping** lä tärje'tä de käm'pēng
campsite	**el campamento ⟨Sp: el cámping⟩** el kämpämen'tō ⟨Sp: el käm'pēng
check-in	**la inscripción** lä ēnskrēpsyōn'
chemical toilet	**el sanitario** el sänētar'yō

clothes drier	**la secadora** lä sekädō'rä
to cook	**cocinar** kōsēnär'
detergent	**el detergente** el deterhen'te
dining room	**el comedor** el kōmedōr'
dinner	**la cena** lä se'nä
double room	**el cuarto ⟨Sp: la habitación⟩ doble** el kōō·är'tō ⟨Sp: lä äbētäsyōn⟩ dō'ble
drinking water	**el agua potable** el ä'gōō·ä pōtä'ble
electricity	**la corriente eléctrica** lä kōryen'te elek'trēkä
foam (insulation) mat	**la estera isotérmica** lä este'rä ēsōter'mēkä
gas	**el gas** el gäs
gas bottle	**la bombona** lä bōmbō'nä
gas canister	**el cartucho** el kärtōō'tshō
gas stove	**el hornillo de gas** el ōrnē'lyō de gäs
hammer	**el martillo** el märtē'lyō
hostel parents	**los responsables del albergue** lōs respōnsä'bles del älber'ge
living room	**la sala de estar** lä sä'lä de estär'
locker	**la consigna** lä kōnsēg'nä
lunch	**el almuerzo, la comida** el älmōō·er'sō, lä kōmē'dä
mosquito net	**el mosquitero** el mōskēte'rō
motor home	**la casa rodante ⟨Sp: el coche-vivienda⟩** lä kä'sä rōdän'te ⟨Sp: el kō'tshe-vēvyen'dä⟩
outlet	**el enchufe** el entshōō'fe
overnight stay	**la pernoctación** lä pernōktäsyōn'

2

room	**el cuarto ⟨Sp: la habitación⟩** el kōō·är'tō ⟨Sp: lä äbētäsyōn'⟩
saucepan	**la olla** lä ō'lyä
to set up	**montar** mōntär'
shower	**la ducha ⟨Mex: la regadera⟩** lä dōō'tshä ⟨Mex: lä regäde'rä⟩
to take a shower	**ducharse** dōōtshär'se
sleeping bag	**el saco de dormir** el sä'kō de dōrmēr'
stove	**el hornillo** el ōrnē'lyō
tent	**la carpa ⟨Sp: la tienda⟩ de campaña** lä kär'pä ⟨Sp: lä tyen'dä⟩ de kämpä'nyä
tent peg	**el piquete** el pēke'te
toilet	**el baño ⟨Mex: el excusado, Sp: el watér,** *in restaurants, etc.:* **los servicios⟩** el bä'nyō ⟨Mex: el ekskōōsä'dō, Sp: el ōō·ä'ter, lōs servē'syōs⟩
to wash	**lavar** lävär'
washing machine	**la lavadora** lä lävädō'rä
washroom (*for clothes*)	**el lavadero** el läväde'rō
water	**el agua** el ä'gōō·ä
water canister	**el bidón de agua** el bēdōn' de ä'gōō·ä
youth group	**el grupo de jóvenes** el grōō'pō de h̲ō'venes
youth hostel	**el albergue juvenil** el älber'ge h̲ōōvenēl'
youth hostel card	**la tarjeta ⟨Sp: el carnet⟩ de alberguista** lä tärh̲e'tä ⟨Sp: el kärnet'⟩ de älbergēs'tä

On the Way

ASKING THE WAY

Excuse me, where is ...?	**Perdone, ¿dónde está ...?** perdō'ne, ¿dōn'de estä' ...?
How do I get to ...?	**¿Por dónde se va a ...?** ¿pōr dōn'de se vä ä ...?
What's the *quickest/ cheapest* way to get to the ...	**¿Cuál es la forma *más rápida/más barata* para ir ...** ¿kōō·äl' es lä fōr'mä *mäs rä'pēdä/mäs bärä'tä* pä'rä ēr ...
train station?	**a la estación de trenes?** ä lä estäsyōn' de tre'nes?
bus station?	**a la estación de bus ⟨Mex: de camión, Sp: de autobuses⟩?** ä lä estäsyōn' de bōōs ⟨Mex: de kämyōn', Sp: outōbōō'ses⟩?
airport?	**al aeropuerto?** äl ä·erōpōō·er'tō?
harbor?	**al puerto?** äl pōō·er'tō?

! **Lo mejor es ir en taxi.** lō mehōr' es ēr en tä'ksē. — It's best to go by taxi.

How do I get to the interstate highway (number...)?	**¿Cómo llego a la autopista (número) ...?** ¿kō'mō lye'gō ä lä outōpēs'tä (nōō'merō ...)?

! **Dé la vuelta.** de lä vōō·el'tä. — Turn around.

! **Todo derecho ⟨Sp: seguido⟩.** tō'dō dere'tshō ⟨Sp: segē'dō⟩. — Straight ahead.

!	**A la derecha.** ä lä dere'tshä.	To the right.
!	**A la izquierda.** ä lä ēskyer'dä.	To the left.
!	**La *primera/segunda* calle a la *izquierda/derecha*.** lä *prēme'rä/ segōōn'dä* kä'lye ä lä *ēskyer'dä/ dere'tshä.*	The *first/second* street to the *left/right.*
!	**En el semáforo.** en el semä'fōrō.	At the traffic light.
!	**Después del cruce.** despōō·es' del 'krōō'se.	After the intersection.
!	**Puede tomar *el bus* ⟨Mex. *el camión*, Sp: *el autobús*⟩/*el metro*.** pōō·e'de tōmär' *el bōōs* ⟨Mex: *el kämyōn'*, Sp: *el outōbōōs'*⟩/*el me'trō.*	You can take the *bus/subway.*

Is this the road to …?	**¿Es ésta la carretera a …?** ¿es es'tä lä kärete'rä ä …?
How far is it?	**¿A qué distancia está?** ¿ä ke dēstän'syä estä'?

!	**Bastante lejos.** bästän'te le'ẖōs.	Rather far.
!	**No está muy lejos.** nō estä mōō'ē le'ẖōs.	Not very far.

3

How many minutes *on foot/by car*? **¿Cuánto se tarda a *pie/en carro* (Sp: *coche*)?** ¿koo·än'tō se tär'dä *ä pye'/en kä'rō* (Sp: *kō'tshe*)?

! **Muy cerca.** moo'ē ser'kä. Nearby.

Could you show me on the map? **Por favor, me lo puede indicar en el mapa.** pōr fävōr', me lō poo·e'de ēndēkär' en el mä'pä?

AT THE BORDER

Passport Control

! **La documentación, por favor.** lä dōkoomentäsyōn' pōr fävōr'. Your papers, please.

! **Su *pasaporte/documento* (Sp: *carnet*) *de identidad*, por favor.** soo *päsäpōr'te/dōkoomen'tō* (Sp: *kärnet'*) *de ēdentēdäd'*, pōr fävōr. Your *passport/ ID card*, please.

! **Su pasaporte está caducado.** soo päsäpōr'te estä' kädookä'dō. Your passport has expired.

? **¿Tiene usted una visa (Sp: un visado)?** ¿tye'ne ooste' oo'nä vē'sä (Sp: oon vēsä'dō)? Do you have a visa?

? **¿Dónde puedo conseguir una visa (Sp: un visado)?** ¿dōn'de poo·e'dō kōnsegēr' oo'nä vē'sä (Sp: oon vēsä'dō)? Where can I get a visa?

Customs

? **¿Tiene algo que declarar?** ¿tye'ne äl'gō ke deklärär'?	Do you have anything to declare?
! **Abra *el portamaletas* ⟨Mex: *la cajuela*/ *la valija*, Sp: *la maleta*⟩, por favor.** ä'brä *el pōrtämäle'täs* ⟨Mex: *lä kähōō·e'lä*/*lä välē'hä*, Sp: *lä mäle'tä*⟩ pōr fävōr'.	Open the *trunk*/*suitcase*, please.
! **Tiene que pagar derechos de aduana.** tye'ne ke pägär' dere'tshōs de ädo͞o·ä'nä.	You'll have to pay duty on that.

At the Border

border	**la frontera** lä frōnte'rä
car registration	**la documentación del automóvil** lä dōko͞omentäsyōn' del outōmō'vēl
customs	**la aduana** lä ädo͞o·ä'nä
customs declaration	**la declaración de aduanas** lä dekläräsyōn' de ädo͞o·ä'näs
date of issue	**la fecha de expedición** lä fe'tshä de ekspedēsyōn'
driver's license	**la licencia de manejar ⟨Sp: el carnet de conducir⟩** lä lēsen'syä de mänehär' ⟨Sp: el kärnet' de kōndo͞osēr'⟩
expired	**caducado** kädo͞okä'dō
first name	**el nombre de pila** el nōm'bre de pē'lä

ID card	**la tarjeta ⟨Sp: el carnet⟩ de identidad** lä tärhe'tä ⟨Sp: el kärnet'⟩ de ēdentēdäd'
invoice	**la factura** lä fäktōō'rä
last name	**el apellido** el äpelyē'dō
nationality sticker *(on license plate)*	**la placa de nacionalidad** lä plä'kä de näsyōnälēdäd'
papers	**la documentación** lä dōkōōmentäsyōn'
passport	**el pasaporte** el päsäpōr'te
passport control	**el control de pasaportes** el kōntrōl' de päsäpōr'tes
to pay duty on	**declarar** deklärär'
place of issue	**el lugar de expedición** el lōōgär' de ekspedēsyōn'
place of residence	**el lugar de residencia** el lōōgär' de resēden'syä
to renew	**renovar** renōvär'
signature	**la firma** lä fēr'mä
travel group	**el grupo de viaje** el grōō'pō de vyä'he
valid	**válido** vä'lēdō
visa	**la visa ⟨Sp: el visado⟩** lä vē'sä ⟨Sp: el vēsä'dō⟩

LUGGAGE

I'd like to *leave my luggage here/pick up my luggage.*	**Quisiera *dejar mi equipaje aquí/recoger mi equipaje.*** kēsy'rä *dehär mē ekēpä'he äkē/rekōher' mē ekēpä'he.*

Can I leave my backpack with you for *one hour/until* ...?	**¿Podría dejarle mi mochila *por una hora/hasta* ...?** ¿pōdrē'ä dehär'le mē mōtshē'lä pōr *o͞o'nä ō'rä/äs'tä*...?
I'd like to check in my luggage to ...	**Quiero facturar este equipaje para ...** kye'rō fäkto͞orär' es'te ekēpä'he pä'rä...
When will it arrive at ...?	**¿Cuándo llegará a ...?** ¿ko͞o än'dō lyegärä' ä...?
My luggage hasn't arrived yet.	**Mi equipaje no ha llegado todavía.** mē ekēpä'he nō ä lyegä'dō tōdävē'ä.
Where is my luggage?	**¿Dónde está mi equipaje?** ¿dōn'de estä' mē ekēpä'he?
These aren't my things.	**Estas no son mis cosas.** es'täs nō sōn mēs kō'säs.
I'm missing a suitcase.	**Me falta una valija ⟨Sp: maleta⟩.** me fäl'tä o͞o'nä välē'hä ⟨Sp: mäle'tä⟩.
My suitcase has been damaged.	**Mi valija ⟨Sp: maleta⟩ ha sido dañada.** me välē'hä ⟨Sp: mäle'tä⟩ ä sē'dō dänyä'dä.
Who can I report it to?	**¿A quién me puedo dirigir?** ¿ä kyen' me poo·e'dō dērēhēr'?

Luggage

backpack	**la mochila** lä mōtshē'lä
bag	**el bolso** el bōl'sō

3

baggage check (office)	**la consigna** lä kōnsēg'nä
baggage check-in	**la facturación de equipaje** lä fäkto͞oräsyōn' de ekēpä'h̲e
baggage claim	**la entrega de equipaje** lä entre'gä de ekēpä'he
baggage claim check	**el resguardo ⟨Sp: el talón⟩** el rezgo͞o·är'dō ⟨Sp: el tälōn'⟩
carry-on luggage	**el equipaje de mano** el ekēpä'h̲e de mä'nō
to check in luggage	**facturar equipaje** fäkto͞orär' ekēpä'he
locker	**la consigna automática** lä kōnsēg'nä outōmä'tēkä
luggage	**el equipaje** el ekēpä'he
to pick up	**recoger** rekōh̲er'
suitcase	**la valija ⟨Sp: maleta⟩** lä välē'h̲ä ⟨Sp: lä mäle'tä⟩
traveling bag	**el bolso de viaje** el bōl'sō de vyä'h̲e

PLANE

Information and Booking

Where is the ... counter?	**¿Dónde está el mostrador de ...?** ¿dōn'de estä' el mōsträdōr' de ...?
When is the next flight to ....?	**¿Cuándo sale el próximo avión para ...?** ¿ko͞o·än'dō sä'le el prō'ksēmō ävyōn' pä'rä ...?

What time *today/ tomorrow* does a plane leave for ... ?	**¿A qué hora sale *hoy/mañana* un avión para ...?** ä ke ō'rä sä'le *oi/ mänyä'nä* o͞on ävyōn' pä'rä ...?
When are we arriving at...?	**¿Cuándo llegaremos a ...?** ¿ko͞o·än'dō lyegäre'mōs ä ...?
How much is the (round trip) fare to ...?	**¿Cuánto cuesta un vuelo (de ida y vuelta) a ...?** ko͞o·än'tō ko͞o·es'tä o͞on vo͞o·e'lō (de ē'dä ē vo͞o·el'tä) ä ...?
I'd like a ticket to ..., ...	**Por favor, un boleto ⟨Sp: un billete⟩ para ..., ...** pōr fävōr', o͞on bōle'tō ⟨Sp: o͞on bēlye'te⟩ pä'rä ...
single	**sólo ida.** sō'lō ē'dä.
round-trip	**ida y vuelta.** ē'dä ē vo͞o·el'tä.
economy class	**clase turista.** klä'se to͞orēs'tä.
business class	**clase preferente.** klä'se preferen'te.
first class	**primera clase.** prēme'rä klä'se.

3

! **Lo siento, pero este vuelo está completo.** lō syen'tō, pe'rō es'te vo͞o·e'lō estä' kōmple'tō. — I'm afraid this flight is booked up.

Are there any *special rates/stand-by seats* available?	**¿Hay *una tarifa especial/plazas stand-by*?** ¿ı *o͞o'nä tärē'fä espesyäl'/ plä'säs estän'-bī*?
I'd like a seat ...	**Quisiera un asiento ...** kēsye'rä o͞on äsyen'tō ...
by the window.	**de ventanilla.** de ventänē'lyä.

on the aisle.	**de pasillo.** de päsē'lyō.
in nonsmoking.	**no fumador.** nō fo͞omädōr'.
in smoking.	**fumador.** fo͞omädōr'.
Where is gate B?	**¿Dónde está la puerta B?** ¿dōn'de estä' lä po͞o·er'tä be?
I'd like to ... my flight.	**Quisiera ... este vuelo.** kēsye'rä ... es'te vo͞o·e'lō.
confirm	**confirmar** kōnfērmär'
cancel	**cancelar** känselär'
change	**cambiar** kämbyär'

On the Plane

Could I have (*another/some more*) ..., please?	**Por favor, ¿podría darme (*otro/mas*) ...?** pōr fävōr', ¿pōdrē'ä där'me (*ō'trō/mäs*) ...?
I feel sick.	**Me encuentro mal.** me enko͞o·en'trō mäl.
Do you have anything for air-sickness?	**¿Tiene un medicamento contra el mareo?** ¿tye'ne o͞on medēkämen'tō kōn'trä el märe'ō?
When are we going to land?	**¿Cuándo aterrizamos?** ¿ko͞o·än'dō äterrēsä'mōs?

Plane

air sick bag	**la bolsa (para el mareo)** lä bōl'sä (pä'rä el märe'ō)
airline	**la compañía aérea** lä kōmpänyē'ä ä·e're·ä
airplane	**el avión** el ävyōn'
airport	**el aeropuerto** el ä·erōpo͞o·er'tō
arrival	**la llegada** lä lyegä'dä
to book	**reservar** reservär'
to cancel	**cancelar** känselär'
to change	**cambiar** kämbyär'
charter flight	**el vuelo chárter** el vo͞o·e'lō tshär'ter
check-in counter	**el mostrador** el mōsträdōr'
to confirm	**confirmar** kōnfērmär'
delay	**el retraso** el reträ'sō
departure	**la salida** lä sälē'dä
exit	**la salida** lä sälē'dä
flight	**el vuelo** el vo͞o·e'lō
flight attendant	**auxiliar de vuelo** ouksēlyär' de vo͞o·e'lō
to fly	**volar** vōlär'
hand luggage	**el equipaje de mano** el ekepä'he de mä'nō
information desk	**el mostrador de información** el mōsträdōr' de ēnfōrmäsyōn'
to land	**aterrizar** äterēsär'
local time	**la hora local** lä ō'rä lōkäl'
nonsmoker	**el no fumador** el nō fo͞omädōr'
return flight	**el vuelo de vuelta** el vo͞o·e'lō de vo͞o·el'tä

scheduled flight	**el vuelo de línea** el vo͞o·e'lō de lē'ne·ä
smoker	**el fumador** el fo͞omädōr'
stopover	**la escala** lä eskä'lä
to take off	**decolar ⟨Sp: despegar⟩** dekōlär' ⟨Sp: despegär⟩
takeoff	**el decolaje ⟨Sp: el despegue⟩** el dekōlä'h̲e ⟨Sp: el despe'ge⟩
ticket	**el boleto ⟨Sp: el billete⟩** el bōle'tō ⟨Sp: bēlye'te⟩

RAIL

Information and Tickets

Where do the trains to ... leave from?	**¿De qué estación salen los trenes para...?** ¿de ke estäsyōn' sälen lōs tre'nes pä'rä?
Where is *the train information office/ the tourist information office*?	**¿Dónde está *la información sobre los trenes/la oficina de información turística*?** ¿dōn'de estä' *lä ēnfōrmäsyōn' sō'bre lōs tre'nes / lä ōfēsē'nä de ēnfōrmäsyōn' to͞orēs'tēkä*?
Where can I find the *baggage check office/ lockers*?	**¿Dónde está *la consigna/la consigna automática*?** ¿dōn'de estä' *lä kōnsēg'nä/ lä kōnsēg'nä outōmä'tēkä*?
When is the *next/last* train to ...?	**¿Cuándo sale el *próximo/último* tren para ...?** ¿ko͞o·än'dō sä'le el *prō'ksēmō/ o͞ol'tēmō* tren pä'rä...?

What time does it get to ... ?	**¿A qué hora llega a ...?** ¿ä ke ō'rä lye'gä ä ...?
When do trains leave for ... ?	**¿Cuándo salen trenes para ...?** ¿kōō·än'dō sä'len tre'nes pä'rä ...?
Do I have to change trains?	**¿Tengo que hacer trasbordo?** ¿teng'gō ke äṣer' träsbōr'dō?
Which platform does the train to ... leave from?	**¿De qué andén sale el tren para ...?** ¿de ke änden' sä'le el tren pä'rä ...?
Which platform does the train from ... arrive at?	**¿En qué andén entra el tren de ...?** ¿en ke änden' en'trä el tren de ...?
What is the fare to ...?	**¿Cuánto cuesta el boleto ⟨Sp: billete⟩ a ...?** ¿kōō·än'tō kōō·e'stä el bōle'tō ⟨Sp: bēye'te⟩ ä ...?
Do I have to pay a supplement?	**¿Hay que pagar suplemento?** ¿ī ke pägär' sōōplemen'tō?
I'd like two tickets to ..., ... please.	**Por favor, dos boletos ⟨Sp: billetes⟩ para ..., ...** pōr fävōr', dōs bōle'tōs ⟨Sp: bēlye'tōs⟩ pä'rä ...
single,	**sólo ida.** sō'lō ē'dä.
round-trip,	**ida y vuelta.** ē'dä ē vōō·el'tä.
first/second class,	**de *primera/segunda* clase.** de *prēme'rä/segōōn'dä* klä'se.

3

for children,	**para niños.** pä'rä nē'nyōs.
for adults,	**para adultos.** pä'rä ädōōl'tōs.
I'd like to reserve a seat on the … train to …, please.	**Por favor, reserve un asiento en el tren para … a las …** pōr fävōr', reser've ōōn äsyen'tō en el tren pä'rä … ä läs …
I'd like a seat …	**Quisiera un asiento …** kēsye'rä ōōn äsyen'tō …
by the window.	**junto a la ventanilla.** h̲ōōn'tō ä lä ventänē'lyä.
in nonsmoking.	**en no fumador.** en nō fōōmädōr'.
in smoking.	**en fumador.** en fōōmädōr'.

Information

Agua potable ä'gōō·ä pōtä'ble	Drinking Water
Andenes ände'nes	Platforms
Consigna kōnsēg'nä	Baggage Check (Office)
Consigna automática kōnsēg'nä outōmä'tēkä	Lockers
Facturación de equipaje fäktōōräsyōn' de ekēpä'h̲e	Baggage Check-In
Información ēnfōrmäsyōn'	Information
Salida sälē'dä	Exit
Servicios servē'syōs	Rest Rooms
Vía vē'ä	Track

INFO On overnight trains in Mexico you can travel in a couchette sleeper with two berths (**cama alta, cama baja**), a sleeping compartment (**camarín**) with toilet and sink, or a bedroom (**alcoba**) with toilet facilities and more space. Stops are frequent and vary in length. Change enough money to last the entire ride.

On the Train

Is this seat taken?	**¿Está libre este asiento?** ¿estä' lē'bre es'te äsyen'tō?
Excuse me, but I believe this is my seat.	**Perdone, creo que éste es mi asiento.** perdō'ne, kre'ō ke es'te es mē äsyen'tō.
Could you help me, please?	**¿Podría usted ayudarme?** ¿pōdrē'ä ōōste' äyōōdär'me?
Do you mind if I *open/close* the window?	**¿Le importa que *abra/cierre* la ventana?** ¿le ēmpōr'tä ke *ä'brä/syer'e* lä ventä'nä?

! **¡Los boletos ⟨Sp: billetes⟩, por favor!** ¡lōs bōle'tōs ⟨Sp: bēlye'tes⟩, pōr fävōr'! — Tickets, please!

How many more stops to...?	**¿Cuántas estaciones quedan para ...?** ¿kōō·än'täs estäsyō'nes ke'dän pä'rä ...?
How long is our stop?	**¿Cuánto tiempo paramos?** ¿kōō·än'tō tyem'pō pärä'mōs?

3

Train

arrival	**la llegada** lä lyegä'dä
baggage car	**el vagón de equipaje** el vägōn' de ekēpä'h̲e
to change trains	**hacer trasbordo** äser' träsbōr'dō
compartment	**el compartimento** el kōmpärtēmen'tō
conductor	**el revisor** el revēsōr'
connection	**el enlace** el enlä'se
departure	**la salida** lä sälē'dä
dining car	**el coche-restaurante** el kō'tshe-restourän'te
to get off *(train)*	**bajar de** bäh̲är' de
to get on *(train)*	**subir a** so͞obēr' ä
to go by train	**ir en tren** ēr en tren
nonsmoking (compartment)	**el no fumador** el nō fo͞omädōr'
occupied	**ocupado** ōko͞opä'dō
platform	**el andén** el änden'
reserved	**reservado** reservä'dō
seat	**el asiento** el äsyen'tō
sleeping compartment *(1-2 beds)*	**el camarín ⟨Sp: el coche-cama⟩** el kämärēn' ⟨Sp: el kō'tshe-kä'mä⟩
smoking (compartment)	**el fumador** el fo͞omädōr'
stop	**la parada** lä pärä'dä
supplement	**el suplemento** el so͞oplemen'tō
ticket	**el boleto ⟨Sp: el billete⟩** el bōle'tō ⟨Sp: el bēlye'te⟩
ticket booth	**la taquilla** lä täkē'lyä

timetable	**el horario** el ōrär'yō
track	**la vía** lä vē'ä
train	**el tren** el tren
train station	**la estación de trenes** lä estäsyōn' de tre'nes
vacant	**libre** lē'bre

BOAT

Information and Booking

When does a *boat/ ferry* leave for ...?	**¿A qué hora sale *un barco/un transbordador* para ...?** ¿ä ke ō'rä sä'le *o͞on bär'kō/o͞on transbōrdädōr'* pa'rä ...?
How long does the crossing to ...... take?	**¿Cuánto dura la travesía a ...?** ¿ko͞o·än'tō do͞o'rä lä trävesē'ä ä ...?
When do we dock in ...?	**¿Cuándo atracamos en ...?** ¿ko͞o·än'dō äträkä'mōs en... ?
When do we have to be on board?	**¿Cuándo tenemos que estar a bordo?** ¿ko͞o·än'dō tene'mōs ke estär' ä bor'do?
I would like ...	**Quisiera ...** kēsye'rä ...
a *first class/tourist class* ticket to ...	**un pasaje de *primera clase/clase turista* para ...** o͞on päsä'he *de prēme'rä klä'se/klä'se to͞orēs'tä* pä'rä ...

3

a single cabin.	**una cabina ⟨Sp: un camarote⟩ individual.** o͞onä käbē'nä ⟨Sp: o͞on kämärō'te⟩ ēndēvēdo͞o·äl'.
I'd like to transport my car.	**Quisiera llevar mi carro ⟨Sp: coche⟩.** kēsye'rä lyevär' mē kä'rō ⟨Sp: kō'tshe⟩
I'd like a ticket for the tour at…	**Quisiera un pasaje para la excursión a las …** kēsye'rä o͞on päsä'he pä'rä lä ekskoo͞rsyōn' ä läs…
Where is… docked?	**¿Dónde está atracado el …?** ¿dōn'de estä' äträkädō el…?

On Board

I'm looking for cabin number…	**Busco la cabina ⟨Sp: el camarote⟩ número …** bo͞os'kō lä käbē'nä ⟨Sp: el kämärō'te⟩ no͞o'merō…
May I change cabins?	**¿Podría cambiar de cabina ⟨Sp: camarote⟩?** ¿pōdrē'ä kämbyär' de käbē'nä ⟨Sp: kämärō'te⟩?
Do you have anything for seasickness?	**¿Tiene usted un medicamento contra el mareo?** ¿tye'ne o͞ostē o͞on medēkä-men'tō kōn'trä el märe'ō?

Boat

2 bed cabin	**la cabina ⟨Sp: el camarote⟩ de dos camas** lä käbē'nä ⟨Sp: el kämärō'te⟩ de dōs kä'mäs

4 bed cabin	**la cabina ⟨Sp: el camarote⟩ de cuatro camas** lä käbē'nä ⟨Sp: el kämärō'te⟩ de ko͞o·ä'trō kä'mäs
berth	**el atracadero** el äträkäde'rō
to board ship	**ir a bordo** ēr ä bōr'dō
cabin	**la cabina ⟨Sp: el camarote⟩** lä käbē'nä ⟨Sp: el kämärō'te⟩
captain	**el capitán** el käpētän'
car ferry	**el transbordador de coches** el tränsbōrdädōr' de kō'tshes
coast	**la costa** lä kōs'tä
crossing	**la travesía** lä trävesē'ä
cruise	**el crucero** el kro͞ose'rō
deck	**la cubierta** lä ko͞obyer'tä
deck chair	**la hamaca** lä ämä'kä
ferry	**el ferry** el fe'rē
harbor	**el puerto** el po͞o·er'tō
hovercraft	**el aerodeslizador** el äe'rōdezlēsädōr'
inside cabin	**la cabina ⟨Sp: el camarote⟩ interior** lä käbē'nä ⟨Sp: el kämärō'te⟩ ēnteryōr'
island	**la isla** lä ēz'lä
lifeboat	**el bote salvavidas** el bō'te sälvävē'däs
life jacket	**el chaleco salvavidas** el tshäle'kō sälvävē'däs
outside cabin	**la cabina ⟨Sp: el camarote⟩ exterior** lä käbē'nä ⟨Sp: el kämärō'te⟩ eksteryōr'
pool	**la alberca ⟨Sp: la piscina⟩** lä älber'kä ⟨Sp: lä pēsē'nä⟩
sea	**el mar** el mär

3

ship	**el barco** el bär'kō
shipping company	**la agencia marítima** lä äh̲en'syä märē'tēmä
shore	**la orilla** lä ōrē'lyä
shore excursion	**la excursión a tierra** lä ekskōōrsyōn' ä tye'rä
steward	**el camarero** el kämäre'rō
sun deck	**la cubierta de sol** lä kōōbyer'tä de sōl
tour	**la excursión** lä ekskōōrsyōn'

CAR, MOTORBIKE AND BIKE

Rentals

I'd like to rent a ... (with automatic).	**Quisiera rentar ⟨Sp: alquilar⟩ ... (con dispositivo automático).** kēsye'rä rentär' ⟨Sp: älkēlär'⟩ ... (kōn dēspōsētē'vō outōmä'tēkō
car	**un carro ⟨Sp: un coche⟩** ōōn kä'rō ⟨Sp: ōōn kō'tshe⟩
four-wheel drive	**un todoterreno** ōōn tōdōtere'nō
a motorcycle	**una moto** ōō'nä mō'tō
motor home	**una casa rodante ⟨Sp: un coche-vivienda⟩** ōō'nä kä'sä rōdän'te ⟨Sp: ōōn kō'tshe-vēvē·en'dä⟩

I'd like to rent a *bicycle/mountain bike.* — **Quisiera rentar ⟨Sp: alquilar⟩ *una bicicleta/una bicicleta de montaña.*** kēsye'rä rentär' ⟨Sp: älkēlär'⟩ *o͞o'nä bēsēkle'tä/o͞o'nä bēsēkle'tä de mōntä'nyä.*

I'd like to rent it for … — **Quisiera rentarla ⟨Sp: alquilarla⟩ …para …** kēsye'rä rentär'lä ⟨Sp: älkēlär'lä⟩ pä'rä…

- tomorrow. — **mañana.** mänyä'nä.
- one day. — **un día.** o͞on dē'lä.
- two days. — **dos días.** dōs dē'äs.
- one week. — **una semana.** o͞o'nä semä'nä.

? **¿Qué tipo de carro ⟨Sp: de coche⟩ quiere usted?** ¿ke tē'pō de kä'rō ⟨Sp: de ko'tshe⟩ kye're o͞oste'? — What kind of car would you like?

How much is it? — **¿Cuánto cuesta?** ¿ko͞o·än'tō ko͞o·es'tä?

? **¿Podría ver su licencia de manejar ⟨Sp: carnet de conducir⟩?** ¿pōdrē'ä ver so͞o lēsen'syä de mänehär' ⟨Sp: kärnet' de kōndo͞osēr'⟩? — Can I see your driver's license, please?

How many kilometers are included in the price? [*1 kilometer = .62 miles*] — **¿Cuántos kilómetros están incluídos en el precio?** ¿ko͞o·än'tōs kēlō'metrōs estän' ēnklo͞o·ē'dōs en el pre'syō?

What kind of gas does it take?	**¿Qué gasolina tengo que poner?** ¿ke gäsōlē'nä teng'gō ke pōner'?
Is comprehensive insurance included?	**¿Está incluído un seguro a todo riesgo?** ¿estä' ēnkloo͞-ē'dō o͞on sego͞o'rō ä tō'dō rē·ez'gō?
What's the deductible?	**¿Cuánto tendría que pagar yo?** ¿ko͞o·än'tō tendrē'ä ke pägär' yō?
When do I have to be back?	**¿Cuándo tengo que estar de vuelta?** ¿ko͞o·än'dō teng'gō ke estär' de vo͞o·el'tä?
Can I turn in the car in …?	**¿Puedo entregar el carro ⟨Sp. coche⟩ en …?** ¿po͞o·e'dō entregär' el kä'rō ⟨Sp: kō'tshe⟩ en …?
I'd also like a helmet.	**Por favor, déme un casco.** pōr fävōr', de'me o͞on käs'kō.

INFO Prepare your car well before driving in Latin America. Take care of all servicing and repairs and follow a few basic precautions, i. e. carrying enough gas and water, a tire pump and patch kit, and tools. Be patient and alert. Watch for pedestrians and animals crossing the road. The stop sign is **alto**, the yield sign is **ceda el paso**; a one-way street has an arrow with the word **circulación** or **tránsito**. A toll road is an **autopista**, also called **cuotas**. You need to insure your vehicle before driving in Mexico.

Parking

Is there a parking lot nearby?	**¿Hay un estacionamiento ⟨Sp: aparcamiento⟩ por aquí cerca?** ¿ī ōōn estäsyōnämyen'tō ⟨Sp: äpärkämyen'tō⟩ pōr äkē' ser'kä?
Is there a guard?	**¿Está vigilado?** ¿estä' vēhēlä'dō?
Is the parking garage open all night?	**¿Está abierto el estacionamiento ⟨Sp. aparcamiento⟩ toda la noche?** ¿estä' äbyer'tō el estäsyōnämyen'tō ⟨Sp: äpärkämyen'tō⟩ tō'dä lä nō'tshe?

Gas Stations, Car Repair

3

Where is the nearest gas station?	**¿Dónde está la gasolinera más próxima?** ¿dōn'de estä' lä gäsōlēne'rä mäs prō'ksēmä?
How far is it to the nearest gas station?	**¿A qué distancia está la gasolinera más próxima?** ¿ä ke dēstän'syä estä' lä gäsōlēne'rä mäs prō'ksēmä?
Fill it up, please.	**Lleno, por favor.** lye'nō, pōr fävōr'.
… *euros/pesetas* worth of…, please.	**Póngame … por … *euros/pesetas.*** pōn'gäme … pōr … *eōō'rōs/pese'täs.*
unleaded	**gasolina sin plomo** gäsōlē'nä sēn plō'mō
diesel fuel	**gasóleo** gäsō'leō
regular	**gasolina normal** gäsōlē'nä nōrmäl

super unleaded	**gasolina súper sin plomo** gäsōlē'nä sōō'per sēn plō'mō
super leaded	**gasolina súper con plomo** gäsōlē'nä sōō'per kōn plō'mō
mixture	**mezcla** mes'klä
Can I pay with this credit card?	**¿Puedo pagar con esta tarjeta de crédito?** ¿pōō·e'dō pägär' kōn es'tä tärhe'tä de kre'dētō?
I'd like *1 liter/ 2 liters* of oil, please. [*1 gallon = 3.8 liters*]	**Quisiera *un litro/ dos litros* de aceite.** kēsye'rä *ōōn lē'trō/dōs lē'trōs* de äse'ēte.
Please change the oil.	**Por favor, cambie el aceite.** pōr fävōr', käm'bye el äse'ēte.

Breakdown and Accidents

Please call ..., quickly!	**Por favor, llame en seguida ...** pōr fävōr', lyä'me en segē'dä ...
an ambulance	**una ambulancia** ōō'nä ämbōō län'syä
the police	**a la policía** ä lä pōlēsē'ä
the fire department	**a los bomberos** ä lōs bōmbe'rōs
I've had an accident.	**He tenido un accidente.** e tenē'dō ōōn äksēden'te.
May I use your phone?	**¿Puedo llamar por teléfono desde aquí?** ¿pōō·e'dō lyämär' pōr tele'fōnō dez'de äkē'?

… people have been (seriously) hurt.	**… personas han resultado heridas (de gravedad).** … persō'näs än resōōltä'dō erē'däs (de grävedäd').
Nobody's hurt.	**Nadie ha resultado herido.** nä'dye ä resōōltä'dō erē'dō.
Please help me.	**Por favor, ayúdeme.** pōr fävōr', äyōō'deme.
I need *some bandages*/ *a first-aid kit.*	**Necesito *vendas*/ *un botiquín.*** nesesē'tō *ven'däs*/ *ōōn bōtēkēn'.*
I'm out of gas.	**El tanque ⟨Sp: depósito⟩ está vacío.** el tän'ke ⟨Sp: depō'sētō⟩ estä' väsē'ō.
Could you …	**¿Podría usted …** ¿pōdrē'ä ōōste' …
give me a lift?	**llevarme en carro ⟨Sp: coche⟩?** lyevär'me en kä'rō ⟨Sp: kō'tshe⟩?
tow my car?	**remolcar mi carro ⟨Sp: coche⟩?** remōlkär' mē kä'rō ⟨Sp: kō'tshe⟩?
send me a tow truck?	**enviarme una grúa?** envyär'me ōō'nä grōō'ä?

INFO On the highway, if a car in front of you signals with the left blinker, this usually means it is safe to pass; a signal with the right blinker means don't pass. Blinking headlights or honking horns by oncoming vehicles usually mean danger ahead of you.

It's not my fault.	**No es culpa mía.** nō es kōōl'pä mē'ä.

I want to call the police.
Quiero que avisemos a la policía.
kye'rō ke ävēse'mōs ä lä pōlēsē'ä.

I had the right-of-way.
Yo tenía preferencia.
yō tenē'ä preferen'syä.

You cut the curve.
Usted ha tomado mal la curva.
o͞oste' ä tōmä'dō mäl lä ko͞or'vä.

You tailgated.
Usted no ha respetado la distancia obligatoria. o͞oste'nō ä respetä'dō lä dēstän'syä ōblēgätō'ryä.

You were speeding.
Usted iba demasiado rápido.
o͞oste' ē'bä demäsyä'dō rä'pēdō.

I was doing … kilometers per hour.
Yo iba a … kilómetros por hora.
yō ē'bä ä … kēlō'metrōs pōr ō'rä.

You damaged …
Ha dañado ⟨Sp: estropeado⟩ …
ä dänyä'dō ⟨Sp: estrōpe·ä'dō⟩ …

May I have *your name and address / your insurance information,* please.
Por favor, déme *su nombre y dirección / su seguro.* pōr fävōr', de'me *so͞o nōm'bre ē dēreksyōn' / so͞o sego͞o'rō.*

Here is *my name and address / my insurance information.*
Aquí tiene *mi nombre y dirección / mi seguro.* äkē' tye'ne *mē nōm'brē ē dēreksyōn' / mē sego͞o'rō.*

Would you be a witness for me?
¿Puede usted servirme de testigo?
¿po͞o·e'de o͞oste' servēr'me de testē'gō?

! **Su documentación, por favor.** sōō dōkōōmentäsyōn', pōr fävōr'. — Your driver's license, registration, and insurance information, please.

Thank you very much for your help. — **Muchas gracias por su ayuda.** mōō'tshäs grä'syäs pōr sōō äyōō'dä.

Do it yourself.

Could you lend me (a)..., please? — **Por favor, ¿podría usted prestarme ...** pōr fävōr', ¿pōdrē'ä ōōste' prestär'-me...?

bicycle repair kit	**un parche?** ōōn pär'tshe?
box end wrench	**una llave tubular ⟨Mex: llave ástria⟩?** ōō'nä lyä've tōōbōōlär' ⟨Mex: lyä've äs'tryä⟩?
drill and bits	**un taladro y brocas?** ōōn tälä'drō ē brō'käs?
wire	**alambre?** äläm'bre?
jack	**un gato?** ōōn gä'tō?
open end wrench	**una llave española?** ōō'nä lyä've espänyō'lä?
lug wrench	**una llave de cruz?** ōō'nä lyä've de krōōs?
pliers	**unas pinzas** ōō'näs pēn'säs?
pump	**una bomba de aire?** ōō'nä bōm'bä de ī're?
screwdriver	**un destornillador ⟨Mex: desarmador⟩?** ōōn destōrnēlyädōr' ⟨Mex: desärmädōr⟩?

3

tools	**herramientas?** erämy·en'täs?
wrench	**una llave inglesa?** o͞o'nä lyä've ēngle'sä?

At the Repair Shop

Where is the nearest ... car repair service ?	**¿Dónde está el taller mecánico (concesionario) de ... más próximo?** ¿dōn'de estä' el tälyer' (kōnsesyōnär'yō) de ... mäs prō'ksēmō?
My car's on the road to ...	**Mi carro ⟨Sp: coche⟩ está en la carretera de ...** mē kä'rō ⟨Sp: kō'tshe⟩ estä' en lä kärete'rä de ...
Can you tow it away?	**¿Puede usted remolcarlo?** ¿po͞o·e'de o͞oste' remōlkär'lō?
Could you take a look at it?	**¿Podría mirarlo?** ¿pōdrē'ä mērär'lō?
... is broken / doesn't work.	***... está roto / no funciona.*** *... estä' rō'tō / nō fo͞onsy·ō'nä.*
My car won't start.	**Mi carro ⟨Sp: coche⟩ no arranca.** mē kä'rō ⟨Sp: kō'tshe⟩ nō äräng'kä.
The battery is dead.	**La batería está descargada.** lä bäterē'ä estä' deskärgä'dä.
The engine sounds funny.	**El motor hace un ruido raro.** el mōtōr' ä'se o͞on ro͞o'ēdō rä'rō.

Just do the essential repairs, please.	**Por favor, haga sólo las reparaciones necesarias.** pōr fävōr', ä'gä sō'lō läs repäräsyō'nes nesesär'yäs.
Can I still drive it?	**¿Puedo seguir circulando?** ¿pōō·e'dō segēr' sērkōōlän'dō?
When will it be ready?	**¿Cuándo estará listo?** ¿kōō·än'dō estärä' lēs'tō?
Do you take checks?	**¿Acepta cheques?** ¿äsep'tä tshe'kes?

Car, Motorbike and Bike

to accelerate	**acelerar** äselerär'
accident	**el accidente** el äksēden'te
automatic (transmission)	**el dispositivo automático** el dēsposētē'vō outōmä'tēkō
battery	**la batería ⟨Mex: el acumulador⟩** lä bäterē'ä ⟨Mex: el äkōōmōōlädōr'⟩
blinker	**el intermitente ⟨Mex. el direcional⟩** el ēntermēten'te ⟨Mex: el dēresyōnäl'⟩
brake	**el freno** el fre'nō
brake light	**la luz de freno** lä lōōs de fre'nō
breakdown	**la falla mecánica ⟨Sp: avería⟩** lä fä'lyä mekä'nēkä ⟨Sp: äverē'ä⟩
bright lights	**la luz larga** lä lōōs lär'gä
broken	**roto ⟨Sp: estropeado⟩** rō'tō ⟨Sp: estrōpe·ä'dō⟩
bumper	**el paragolpes ⟨Mex: la defensa, Sp: el parachoques⟩** el pärägōl'pes ⟨Mex: lä defen'sä, Sp: el pärätshō'kes⟩

3

car	**el carro ⟨Sp: el coche⟩** el kä'rō ⟨Sp: el kō'tshe⟩
carburetor	**el carburador** el kärbo͞orädōr'
car repair service	**el taller mecánico** el tälyer' mekä'nēkō
catalytic converter	**el catalizador** el kätälēsädōr'
chains	**las cadenas f/pl** läs käde'näs
child seat	**el asiento para niños** el äsyen'tō pä'rä nē'nyōs
clutch	**el cloche ⟨Sp: embrague⟩** el klō'tshe ⟨Sp: el embrä'ge⟩
distilled water	**el agua destilada** el ä'go͞o·ä destēlä'dä
driver's license	**la licencia de manejar ⟨Sp: el carnet de conducir⟩** lä lēsen'syä de mänehär' ⟨Sp: el kärnet' de kōndo͞osēr'⟩
dynamo	**la dínamo** lä dē'nämō
emergency brake	**el freno de mano** el fre'nō de mä'nō
emergency triangle	**el triángulo de emergencia** el trē·äng'go͞olō de emerhen'syä
engine	**el motor** el mōtōr'
exhaust	**el escape** el eskä'pe
fanbelt	**la banda ⟨Sp: correa⟩ del ventilador** lä bän'dä ⟨Sp: kōre'ä⟩ del ventēlädōr'
fender	**el guardabarros** el go͞o·ärdäbä'rōs
first-aid kit	**el botiquín** el bōtēkēn'
four-wheel drive	**el vehículo todoterreno** el ve·ē'ko͞olō tōdōtere'nō
gas	**la gasolina ⟨Arg: la nafta⟩** lä gäsōlē'nä ⟨Arg: lä näf'tä⟩

gas station	**la gasolinera ⟨Co: la bomba, Pe: el grifo⟩** lä gäsōlēne'rä ⟨Co: lä bōm'bä, Pe: el grē'fō⟩
gasket	**el empaque ⟨Sp: la junta⟩** el empä'ke ⟨Sp: lä h̲o͞on'tä⟩
gear	**el engrane ⟨Sp: la marcha⟩** el engrä'ne ⟨Sp: lä mär'tshä⟩
headlights	**el faro** el fä'rō
helmet	**el casco** el käs'kō
highway	**el autopista** el outōpēs'tä
horn	**la bocina** lä bōsē'nä
hubcap	**el tapacubos** el täpäko͞o'bōs
idle	**el punto muerto** el po͞on'tō mo͞o·er'tō
ignition	**el encendido** el ensendē'dō
ignition cable	**el cable de encendido** el kä'ble de ensendē'dō
injured	**herido** erē'dō
inner tube	**la cámara ⟨Mex: el tubo⟩ de aire** lä kä'merä ⟨Mex: el to͞o'bō⟩ de ī're
insurance	**el seguro** el sego͞o'rō
kilometer	**el kilómetro** el kēlō'metrō
license plate	**la matrícula** lä mätrē'ko͞olä
low beams	**la luz de cruce** lä lo͞os de kro͞o'se
main road	**la carretera** lä kärrete'rä
motorcycle	**la moto** lä mō'tō
no parking	**prohibido estacionar ⟨Sp: aparcar⟩** prō·ēbē'dō estäsyōnär' ⟨Sp: äpärkär'⟩
oil	**el aceite para el motor** el äse'ēte pä'rä el mōtōr'

3

oil change **el cambio de aceite** el käm'byō de äse'ēte

to park **estacionar ⟨Sp: aparcar⟩** estäsyōnär' ⟨Sp: äpärkär'⟩

parking disk **el disco de estacionamiento ⟨Sp: aparcamiento⟩** el dēs'kō de estäsyōnämyen'tō ⟨Sp: äpärkämyen'tō⟩

parking lights **la luz de población** lä lōōs de pōbläsyōn'

parking meter **el parquímetro** el pärkē'metrō

pressure **la presión de las llantas ⟨Sp: los neumáticos⟩** lä presyōn' de läs lyän'täs ⟨Sp: lōs ne·ōōmä'tēkōs⟩

rear-end collision **el accidente de alcance** el äksēden'te de älkän'se

to repair **reparar** repärär'

reserve fuel can **el tarro ⟨Sp: bidón⟩ de reserva** el tä'rrō ⟨Sp: bēdōn'⟩ de reser'vä

right of way **la preferencia de paso** lä preferen'syä de pä'sō

seat belt **el cinturón de seguridad** el sēntōōrōn' de segōōrēdäd'

shock absorber **el amortiguador** el ämōrtēgōō·ädōr'

spare part **la pieza de repuesto ⟨Sp: recambio⟩** lä pye'sä de repōōe'stō ⟨Sp: rekäm'byō⟩

spare tire **la llanta de repuesto ⟨Sp: el neumático de recambio⟩** lä lyän'tä de repōō·es'tō ⟨Sp: el ne'ōōmä'tēkō de rekäm'byō⟩

spark plug **la bujía** lä bōōh̲ē'ä

starter	**la marcha ⟨Sp: el arranque⟩** lä mär'tshä ⟨Sp: el ärän'ke⟩
steering	**la dirección** lä dēreksyōn'
tail light	**la luz trasera** lä lōōs träse'rä
tire	**la llanta ⟨Sp: el neumático⟩** lä lyäntä ⟨Sp: el ne·ōōmä'tēkō⟩
to tow away	**remolcar** remōlkär'
tow rope	**el cable de remolque** el kä'ble de remōl'ke
tow truck	**la grúa** lä grōō'ä
transmission	**la transmisión ⟨Sp: el cambio de marchas⟩** lä tränsmēsyōn' ⟨Sp: el käm'byō de mär'tshäs⟩
unleaded	**sin plomo** sēn plō'mō
valve	**la válvula** lä väl'vōōlä
water	**el agua** el ä'gōō·ä
wheel	**la rueda** lä rōō·e'dä
windshield wiper	**el limpiaparabrisas** el lēmpyäpäräbrē'säs

BUS, SUBWAY, TAXI

Bus and Subway

Where's the nearest subway station?	**¿Dónde está la próxima parada de metro?** ¿dōn'de estä' lä prō'ksēmä pärä'dä de me'trō?

Where does the bus to… stop?	**¿Dónde para el bus ⟨Mex: el camión, Sp: el autobús⟩ para …?** ¿dōn'de pä'rä el bo͞os ⟨Mex: el kämyōn', Sp: el outōbo͞os'⟩ pä'rä…?
Which subway goes to…?	**¿Qué metro va a …?** ¿ke me'trō vä ä…?

! **La línea…** lä 'lē'ne·ä… The… line.

Where do the buses to… leave from?	**¿De qué estación salen los buses para …?** ¿de ke estäsyōn' sä'len lōs bo͞o'ses pä'rä…?

INFO Latin America is extensively served by buses. Wherever there's a road, there's a bus. Sometimes the more high-speed, air-conditioned buses are called **Pullman.** You can get a bus at the **Central de Autobuses.** City buses usually have **servicio urbano** written on them. Large Mexican cities have minibuses (**peseros, colectivos**) running along prescribed routes, picking up and dropping off passengers as they go along.

When is the next *bus/ subway* to …?	**¿A qué hora sale el próximo *bus/ metro* para …?** ¿ä ke ō'rä sä'le el prō'ksēmō *bo͞os/me'trō* pä'rä …?
When does the last *bus/subway* leave for …?	**¿Cuándo sale el último *bus/metro* para …?** ¿ko͞o·än'dō sä'le el o͞ol'tēmō *bo͞os/me'trō* pä'rä …?

Does this bus leave at the same time on *Saturday/Sunday*?

¿Sale este bus los *sábados/domingos* a la misma hora? ¿sä'le es'te bo͞os lōs *sä'bädōs/dōmēng'gōs* ä lä mēz'mä ō'rä?

Where can I buy a ticket?

¿Dónde se compran los boletos ⟨Sp: los billetes⟩? ¿dōn'de se kōm'prän lōs bōle'tōs ⟨Sp: lōs bēlye'tes⟩?

Are there ... multiple-ride tickets for the *bus/subway*?

¿Hay boletos ⟨Sp: billetes⟩ rebajados para *bus/metro*? ¿ī bōle'tōs ⟨Sp: bēye'tes⟩ rebähä'dōs pä'rä *bo͞os/me'trō*?

I'd like a ticket to ..., please.

Por favor, un boleto ⟨Sp: billete⟩ para ... pōr fävōr', o͞on bōle'tō ⟨Sp: bēye'te⟩ pä'rä ...

Does this *bus/subway* go to ...?

¿Va este *bus/metro* a ...? ¿vä es'te *bo͞os/me'trō* ä ...?

Do I have to change for ...?

¿Tengo que cambiar de línea para ir a ...? ¿teng'gō ke kämbyär' de lē'ne·ä pä'rä ēr ä ...?

Could you tell me where I have to *get off/change*, please?

Por favor, dígame dónde tengo que *bajar/cambiar*. pōr fävōr', dē'gäme dōn'de teng'gō ke *bähär'/kämbyär'*.

Taxi!

Where is the taxi stand?

¿Dónde está la parada de taxis? ¿dōn'de estä' lä pärä'dä de tä'ksēs?

3

Could you order a taxi for me for …?	**¿Podría pedirme un taxi para…?** ¿pōdrē·ä pedēr'me o͞on tä'ksē pä'rä…?
Could you take me…, please?	**Por favor, lléveme…** pōr fävōr', lye'veme…
to the station	**a la estación** ä lä estäsyōn'
to the airport	**al aeropuerto** äl ä·erōpo͞o·er'tō
to the… Hotel	**al hotel…** äl ōtel'…
downtown	**al centro de la ciudad** äl sen'trō de lä syo͞odäd'
How much is it to …?	**¿Cuánto cuesta a …?** ¿ko͞o·än'tō ko͞o·es'tä ä …?
Please put the meter at zero.	**Por favor, ponga el taxímetro a cero.** pōr fävōr', pōng'gä el täksē'metrō' ä se'rō.
Could you *wait/stop* here (for a minute), please?	***Espere/Pare*** **(un momento) aquí, por favor.** *espe're/pä're* (o͞on mōmen'tō) äkē', pōr fävōr'.

Bus, Subway, Taxi

bus	**el bus ⟨Mex: el camión, Sp: el autobús⟩** el bo͞os ⟨Mex: el kämyōn', Sp: el outōbo͞os'⟩
bus stop	**la parada de bus ⟨Mex: camión, Sp: autobús⟩** lä pärä'dä de bo͞os ⟨Mex: kämyōn', Sp: outōbo͞os'⟩
bus terminal	**la estación de autobuses** lä estäsyōn' de outōbo͞o'ses

to cancel	**cancelar** känselär'
to change	**cambiar** kämbyär'
departure	**la salida** lä sälē'dä
direction	**la dirección** lä dēreksyōn'
downtown	**el centro de la ciudad** el sen'trō de lä syo͞odäd'
driver	**el conductor** el kōndo͞oktōr'
fare	**el precio del boleto ⟨Sp: billete⟩** el pre'syō del bōle'tō ⟨Sp: bēlye'te⟩
to get off	**bajar (de)** bähär' (de)
to get on	**subir (a)** so͞obēr' (ä)
receipt	**el recibo** el resē'bō
schedule	**el horario** el ōrär'yō
stop	**la parada** lä pärä'dä
to stop	**parar** pärär'
subway	**el metro** el me'trō
taxi	**el taxi** el tä'ksē
taxi stand	**la parada de taxis** lä pärä'dä de tä'ksēs
terminal	**la terminal** lä termēnäl'
ticket	**el boleto ⟨Sp: el billete⟩** el bōle'tō ⟨Sp: el bēlye'te⟩
ticket checker	**el revisor ⟨Mex. el auditor⟩** el revesōr' ⟨Mex: el oudētōr'⟩
ticket vending machine	**la máquina expendedora de boletos ⟨Sp: billetes⟩** lä mä'kēnä ekspendedō'rä de bōle'tōs ⟨Sp: bēlye'tes⟩
weekly ticket	**el boleto ⟨Sp: billete⟩ semanal** el bōle'tō ⟨Sp: bēlye'te⟩ semänäl'

HITCHHIKING

I'm on my way to...	**Quisiera ir a...** kēsye'rä ēr ä...
Where are you going?	**¿Adónde va usted?** ¿ädōn'de vä ōōste'?
Could you give me a ride (as far as...)?	**¿Me puede llevar (hasta)...?** ¿me pōō·e'de lyevär' (ä'stä)...?

INFO In Mexico hitchhiking is called **viajar por aventón.** If you want someone to give you a ride you can ask **¿Me da un aventón a...?**

? **¿Dónde se quiere bajar?** ¿dōn'de se kye're bähär'? — Where do you want to get out?

Could you let me out here, please?	**Por favor, déjeme aquí.** pōr fävōr, de'heme äkē'.
Thanks for the lift.	**Muchas gracias por llevarme.** 'mōō'tshäs grä'syäs pōr lyevär'me.

Food and Drink

CARTA kär'tä MENU

Aperitivos, entremeses y ensaladas *äperētē' vōs, entreme' ses ē ensälä' däs*	*Appetizers and salads*
las aceitunas läs äseytōō'näs	olives
el aguacate el ägōō·äkä'te	avocado
las alcachofas salteadas läs älkätshō'fäs sälte·ä'däs	salted artichokes
las anchoas läs äntshō'äs	anchovies
los antojitos (Mex.) lōs äntōhē'tōs	Mexican hor d'oeuvres
los berberechos al natural lōs berbere¥tshōs äl nätōōräl'	cockles in their own juice
los boquerones fritos lōs bōkerō'nes frē'tōs	fried small sardines
la butifarra lä bōōtēfä'rä	pork sausage
los camarones (Mex.) lōs kämärō'nes	shrimps
la carne en brochete lä kär'ne en brōtshe'te	shish kabobs
las carnes frías läs kär'nes frē'äs	cold cuts
el ceviche el sevē'tshe	marinated raw fish
los chicharrones (Mex.) lōs tshētshärō'nes	pig cracklings
el chorizo el tshōrē'sō	spicy link sausage
las croquetas läs krōke'täs	croquettes
la empanada lä empänä'dä	meat pastry

la ensalada lä ensälä'dä	salad
- mixta mēks'tä	mixed salad
la ensaladilla rusa (Sp) lä ensälädē'lyä rōō'sä	vegetable salad with mayonnaise
los fiambres lōs fē·äm'bres	cold cuts
las gambas al ajillo (Sp.) läs gäm'bäs äl äh̲ē'lyō	shrimps in garlic sauce
el guacamole (Mex.) el gōōäkämō'le	avocado dip
el jamón serrano (Sp.) el h̲ämōn' serä'nō	Serrano ham
los mejillones al vapor lōs meh̲ēlyō'nes äl väpōr'	steamed mussels
los pimientos fritos lōs pēmyen'tōs frē'tōs	fried peppers
los pinchos morunos lōs pēn'tshōs mōrōō'nōs	shish kabobs
el queso el ke'sō	cheese
la quesadilla (Mex.) lä kesädē'lyä	tortilla with melted cheese

Sopas y guisos *sō'päs ē gē'sōs* — *Soups and Stews*

el caldo el käl'dō	broth
el gazpacho el gäspä'tshō	cold tomato soup
el pote gallego (Sp.) el pō'te gälye'gō	meat and vegetable stew
la sopa lä sō'pä	soup
- de ajo de ä'h̲ō	garlic soup

4

- de fideos de fēde'ōs	noodle soup
- de pescado de peskä'dō	fish soup
- de pollo de pō'lyō	chicken soup
- de verduras de verdo͞o'räs	vegetable soup

Arroz *ärōs'* *Rice*

el arroz el ärōs'	rice
- a la cubana ä lä ko͞obä'nä	- with egg and banana
- a la marinera ä lä märēne'rä	- with fish
- blanco bläng'kō	white rice
- con pollo kōn pō'lyō	- with chicken
la paella lä pä·e'lyä	rice with seafood and vegetables

Especialidades mexicanas *espesyälēdäd' es meh̲ēkä'näs* *Mexican specialities*

las carnitas läs kärnē'täs	pork cooked in a cauldron served with tortillas and chiles
el chile relleno el tshē'le relye'nō	stuffed poblano chile
la enchilada lä entshēlä'dä	rolled tortilla in salsa with choice of filling
los frijoles refritos lōs freh̲ō'les refrē'tōs	refried beans
el menudo el meno͞o'dō	tripe soup
el mole el mō'le	sauce made of chocolate, chile and spices

el taco el tä'kō	folded tortilla with choice of filling
los tamales läs tämä'les	steamed corn dough wrapped in corn husk and filled
la tortilla lä tōrtē'lyä	round flat cakes of corn flour

Platos de carnes *plä'tōs de kär'nes* — *Meat dishes*

el bistec el bēstek'	steak
el carnero el kärne'rō	mutton
el cochino ⟨Sp: el cerdo⟩ el kōtshē'nō ⟨Sp: el ser'dō⟩	pork
el cochinillo el kōtshēnē'lyō	suckling pig
el conejo el kōne'h̲ō	rabbit
el cordero el kōrde'rō	lamb
el hígado el hē'gädō	liver
la res ⟨Sp: la vaca⟩ lä res ⟨Sp: lä vä'kä⟩	beef
la ternera lä terne'rä	veal
el venado el venä'dō	venison
las albóndigas en tomate läs älbōn'dēgäs en tōmä'te	meatballs in tomato sauce
el bistec con papas ⟨Sp: patatas⟩ el bēstek' kōn pä'päs ⟨Sp: pätä'täs⟩	steak and potatoes
la brocheta de carne lä brōtshe'tä de kär'ne	shish kebab
el cabrito al vino blanco el käbrē'tō äl vē'nō bläng'kō	goat in white wine

4

la carne asada lä kär'ne äsä'dä grilled meat

la carne machada lä kär'ne mätshä'dä cured, dried and shredded beef

la chuleta lä tshōōle'tä chop

el conejo al ajillo el kōne'h̲ō äl äh̲ē'lyō rabbit in garlic sauce

el cordero asado el kōrde'rō äsä'dō roast lamb

las costillas de cordero läs kōstē'lyäs de kōrde'rō lamb ribs

el escalope el eskälō'pe breaded cutlet

el estofado de cordero el estōfä'dō de kōrde'rō lamb stew

el filete de cerdo empanado el fēle'te de ser'dō empänä'dō breaded pork filet

el filete de ternera el fēle'te de terne'rä veal filet

el lomo el lō'mō loin

el salpicón el sälpēkōn' cold cooked meat with chiles

el solomillo el sōlōmē'lyō sirloin

Aves *ä'ves* *Fowl/Poultry*

las codornices a la plancha läs kōdōrnē'ses ä lä plän'tshä grilled quails

el pavo ⟨Mex: el guajalote⟩ asado el pä'vō ⟨Mex: el gōōäh̲älō'te⟩ äsä'dō roast turkey

la pechuga de pollo lä petshōō'gä de pō'lyō chicken breast

las perdices rellenas	läs perdē'ses relye'näs	stuffed partridges
los pichones a la española	lōs pētshō'nes ä lä espänyō'lä	young pigeons Spanish style
el pollo al ajillo	el pō'lyō äl äh̲ē'lyō	chicken in garlic sauce
el pollo asado	el pō'lyō äsä'dō	roast chicken
el pollo en salsa	el pō'lyō en säl'sä	chicken in gravy
el pollo pibil	el pō'lyō pēbēl'	chicken baked in banana leaves

Pescado *peskä'dō* *Fish*

el anguila a la donostiarra	el äng·gē'lä ä lä dōnostyä'rä	Basque-style eel
el atún encebollado	el ätōōn' ensebōlyä'dō	tuna with onions
el bacalao al pil-pil	el bäkälä'ō äl pēl-pēl	dried cod in oil and garlic
el besugo al horno	el besōō'gō äl ōr'nō	oven roasted sea bream
los boquerones	lōs bōkerō'nes	small sardines
la caballa asada (Sp.)	lä käba'lyä äsä'dä	grilled mackerel
la cabrilla (Mex.)	lä käbrē'lyä	(type of) rock fish
los calamares	lōs kälämä'res	squid
la dorada a la sal (Sp.)	lä dōrä'dä ä lä säl	dorado in a salt crust

4

el huachinango a la veracruzana el o͞o·ätshēnäng'gō ä lä veräkro͞o'sä'nä	red snapper Veracruz style
el lenguado el leng·go͞o·ä'dō	sole
la lubina lä lo͞obē'nä	smallmouth bass
la merluza en salsa verde lä merlo͞o'sä en säl'sä ver'de	hake in green sauce
el mero el me'rō	grouper
los pescados fritos lōs peskä'dōs frē'tōs	fried fish
el pez espada el pes espä'dä	swordfish
el rape el rä'pe	anglerfish
el robalo el rōbä'lō	snook
el salmón a la plancha el sälmōn' ä lä plän'tshä	grilled salmon
las sardinas läs särdē'näs	sardines
la sierra (Mex.) lä sye'rä	Spanish mackerel
el tiburón el tēbo͞orōn'	shark
la trucha rellena de jamón lä tro͞o'tshä relye'nä de h̲ämōn'	trout stuffed with ham

Mariscos *märēs'kōs* *Seafood*

el abulón (Mex.) el äbo͞olōn'	abelone
las almejas läs älme'h̲äs	clams
el atún el äto͞on'	tuna
el bogavante el bōgävän'te	lobster
los camarones gigantes lōs kämärō'nes h̲ēgän'tes	prawns

los cangrejos de mar lōs käng·gre'h̲ōs de mär	crabs
la cazuela de mariscos lä käso͞o·e'lä de märēs'kōs	seafood stew
las cigalas läs sēgä'läs	Norway lobster
la langosta lä läng·gōs'tä	lobster
los langostinos lōs läng·gōstē'nōs	prawns
los mejillones rellenos lōs meh̲ēlyō'nes relye'nōs	stuffed mussels
los ostiones ⟨Sp. ostras⟩ en su concha lōs ōstyō'nes ⟨Sp: ōs'träs⟩ en so͞o kōn'tshä	oysters on the half shell
el pulpo el po͞ol'pō	octopus
el salpicón de mariscos el sälpēkōn' de märēs'kōs	seafood salad

Verduras y legumbres *verdo͞o'räs ē lego͞om'bres*	***Vegetables***
las acelgas läs äsel'gäs	Swiss chard
el aguacate el ägo͞o·äkä'te	avocado
las alcachofas läs älkätshō'fäs	artichoke
el ajo el ä'h̲ō	garlic
el apio el ä'pyō	celery
la batata lä bätä'tä	sweet potato
las berenjenas fritas läs berenh̲e'näs frē'täs	fried eggplant
los calabacines rellenos lōs käläbäsē'nes relye'nōs	stuffed zucchini

4

la calabaza lä käläbä'sä — pumpkin
la cebolla lä sebō'lyä — onion
los champiñones al ajillo lōs tshämpēnyō'nes äl äh̲ē'lyō — mushrooms in garlic sauce
los chícharos ⟨Sp: los guisantes⟩ lōs tshē'tshärōs ⟨Sp: lōs gēsän'tes⟩ — peas
el chile el tshē'le — chile
  - jalapeño (en escabeche) h̲äläpe'nyō (en eskäbe'tshe) — hot chile (pickled)
  - poblano pōblä'nō — mild dark green chile
la col lä kōl — cabbage
la coliflor refrita lä kōlēflōr' refrē'tä — fried cauliflower
los ejotes ⟨Sp: las judías verdes⟩ lōs eh̲ō'tes ⟨Sp: läs h̲o͞odē'äs ver'des⟩ — green beans
la endibia lä endē'byä — endive
la escarola lä eskärō'lä — escarole
los espárragos lōs espärä'gōs — asparagus
las espinacas läs espēnä'käs — spinach
los frijoles ⟨Sp: las judías⟩ lōs frēh̲ō'les ⟨Sp: läs h̲o͞odē'äs⟩ — beans
los garbanzos lōs gärbän'sōs — chick peas
el jitomate (Mex.) el hētōmä'te — beefsteak tomato
la lechuga lä letsho͞o'gä — lettuce
las lentejas läs lente'h̲äs — lentils
el maíz el mä·ēs' — corn

los nopalitos (Mex.) lōs nōpälē'tōs	young cactus leaves
las papas ⟨Sp: patatas⟩ läs pä'päs ⟨Sp: pätä'täs⟩	potatoes
- fritas frē'täs	French fries
el pepino el pepē'nō	cucumber
los pimientos lōs pēmyen'tōs	bell peppers
el tomate el tōmä'te	tomato
la zanahoria lä sänä·ōr'yä	carrot

Huevos *o͞o·e'vōs* — *Egg dishes*

los huevos lōs o͞o·e'vōs	eggs
- duros do͞o'rōs	hard-boiled
- fritos frē'tōs	fried
- pasados por agua päsä'dōs pōr ä'go͞oä	soft-boiled
- rancheros räntshe'rōs	Mexican ranch style
- revueltos revo͞o·el'tōs	scrambled
el omelet (Mex.) el ōmelet'	omelette
la tortilla española (Sp.) lä tōrtē'lyä espänyō'lä	potato omelette
la tortilla de jamón (Sp.) lä tōrtē'lyä de h̲ämōn'	ham omelette

Modos de preparación *mō'dōs de prepäräsyōn'* — *Methods of Preparation*

adobado ädōbä'dō	marinated
ahumado ä·o͞omä'dō	smoked

asado äsä'dō	roasted
asado a la parilla äsä'dō ä lä pärrē'lyä	grilled
cocido kōsē'dō	boiled
cocido al vapor kōsē'dō äl väpōr'	steamed
empanado empänä'dō	breaded
estofado estōfä'dō	stewed
frito frē'tō	fried
hecho en casa e'tshō en kä'sä	homemade
horneado ōrneä'dō	baked
relleno relye'nō	stuffed
tostado tōstä'dō	toasted

Postres pōs'tres Desserts

el arroz con leche el ärōs' kōn le'tshe	rice pudding
la crema catalana (Sp.) lä kre'mä kätälä'nä	caramel custard
la cuajada (Sp.) lä kōō·äẖä'dä	flavored thickened milk
el dulce de leche el dōōl'se de le'tshe	sweet milk dessert
el dulce de membrillo el dōōl'se de membrē'lyō	quince jelly
el flan el flän	caramel custard
las fresas con crema ⟨Sp: nata⟩ läs fre'säs kōn kre'mä ⟨Sp: nä'tä⟩	strawberries and whipped cream

la fruta del tiempo lä fro͞o'tä del tyem'pō	fruit in season
el helado el elä'dō	ice cream
el merengue el mereng'ge	meringue
las natillas läs nätē'lyäs	egg custard
el tocino del cielo el tōsē'nō del sye'lō	thick egg custard

Frutas *fro͞o'täs* *Fruit*

el albaricoque (Sp.) el älbärēkō'ke	apricot
la banana lä bänä'nä	banana
las cerezas läs sere'säs	cherries
el damasco ⟨Mex: el chabacano⟩ el dämäs'kō ⟨Mex: el tchäbäkä'nō⟩	apricot
la chirimoya lä tshērēmō'yä	sour sop
la ciruela lä sero͞o·e'lä	plum
el coco el kō'kō	coconut
el coctel ⟨Sp: la macedonia⟩ de frutas el kōktel' ⟨Sp: lä mäsedō'nyä⟩ de fro͞o'täs	fruit salad
el durazno el do͞oräs'nō	peach
las fresas läs fre'säs	strawberries
la granada lä gränä'dä	pomegranate
la guayaba lä go͞o·äyä'bä	guava
los higos lōs ē'gōs	figs
el mango el mäng'gō	mango
la manzana lä mänsä'nä	apple

4

el melocotón (Sp.) el melōkōtōn'	peach
el melón el melōn'	melon
la naranja lä närän'h̲ä	orange
la papaya lä päpä'yä	papaya
la pera lä pe'rä	pear
el ananás ⟨Sp: la piña⟩ el änänäs' ⟨Sp: lä pē'nyä⟩	pineapple
el plátano (Sp.) el plä'tänō	banana
el pomelo el pōme'lō	grapefruit
la sandía ⟨Co: la patilla⟩ lä sändē'ä ⟨Cō: lä pätē'lyä⟩	watermelon
la toronja (Mex.) lä tōrōn'h̲ä	grapefruit
la uva lä o͞o'vä	grape

Dulces do͞ol'ses *Pastries*

el bizcocho el bēēskō'tshō	pound cake
los buñuelos (Mex.) lōs bo͞onyo͞o·e'lōs	deep fried pastry with sugar and honey
los buñuelos de viento (Sp.) lōs bo͞onyo͞o·e'lōs de vyen'tō	cream puff
los churros lōs tsho͞o'rōs	deep fried pastry dusted with sugar
la ensaimada (Sp.) lä ensīmä'dä	(type of) Danish
la galleta lä gälye'tä	cookie
la tarta lä tär'tä	cake
las torrijas (Sp.) läs tōrē'h̲äs	(type of) French toast
el turrón el to͞orōn'	nougat bar

INFO In addition to omnipresent soft drinks, there is a wide range of fresh fruit juices through most of Latin America, including such exotic ones as tamarind juice **jugo de tamarindo** and guava juice **jugo de guayaba**. Beer is not as light as North American beer. Mexico is famous for its **tequila,** from which the well-known **margarita** cocktails are made. Chile has become world famous for its wines. When you order drinks, you can ask for them in a can, **en lata,** and without ice, **sin hielo.**

BEBIDAS bebē'däs BEVERAGES

Vinos *vē'nōs* *wine*

el vino el vē'nō — wine
- **blanco** bläng'kō — white wine
- **tinto** tēn'tō — red wine
- **rosado** rōsä'dō — rosé
- **espumoso** espōōmō'sō — sparkling wine
- **de la casa** de lä kä'sä — house wine

la sangría lä säng·grē'ä — wine punch
la sidra lä sē'drä — cider
el champán el tshämpän' — champagne
el cava el kä'vä — sparkling wine
- **dulce** dōōl'se — sweet
- **seco** se'kō — dry

4

Cerveza *serve'sä*	*Beer*
la cerveza lä serve'sä	beer
- negra ne'grä	dark beer
- clara ⟨Sp: rubia⟩ klärä ⟨Sp: ro͞o'byä⟩	light beer
- de barril de bärēl'	draft beer
la jarra de cerveza lä h̲ä'rä de serve'sä	pitcher of beer
el botellín el bōtelyēn'	small bottle of beer
la caña lä kä'nyä	glass of beer
Otras bebidas alcohólicas *ō'träs bebē'däs älkō·ō'lēkäs*	*Other alcoholic drinks*
el aguardiente el ägo͞o·ärdyen'te	sugarcane-based clear liquor
el coñac el kōnyäk'	cognac, brandy
el jerez el h̲eres'	sherry
el mezcal el meskäl'	mescal
el pisco el pēs'kō	grape-based clear liquor
el ron el rōn	rum
la tequila lä tekē'lä	tequila
Bebidas no alcohólicas *bebē'däs nō älkō·ō'lēkäs*	*Non-alcoholic drinks*
el agua el ä'go͞o·ä	water
el agua mineral el ä'go͞o·ä mēneräl'	mineral water
- con gas kōn gäs	carbonated

- **sin gas** sēn gäs — still

el batido el bätē'dō — milk shake
el granizado el gränēsä'dō — iced beverage
la horchata (Sp.) lä ōrtshä'tä — almond milk
los licuados (Mex.) lōs lēko͞o·ä'dōs — shakes
el jugo ⟨Sp: el zumo⟩ el ho͞o'gō ⟨Sp: el so͞o'mō⟩ — juice

- **de manzana** de mänsä'nä — apple juice
- **de naranja** de närän'hä — orange juice
- **de tomate** de tōmä'te — tomato juice

Bebidas calientes *bebē'däs kälyen'tes* — *Hot drinks*

el café el käfe' — coffee

- **con leche** kōn le'tshe — coffee with milk
- **solo** sō'lō — black coffee

el carajillo (Sp.) el kärähē'lyō — coffee with a dash of brandy
el chocolate el tshōkōlä'te — hot chocolate
el cortado el kōrtä'dō — espresso coffee with a little milk
la infusión de hierbabuena lä ēnfo͞osyōn' de yerbäbo͞o·e'nä — mint tea
la leche lä le'tshe — milk
la manzanilla lä mänzänē'lyä — chamomile tea
el té el te — hot tea

- **con limón** kōn lēmōn' — with lemon

4

INFORMATION

Is there ... near here?	**¿Dónde hay ... por aquí cerca?** ¿dōn'de ī pōr äkē' ser'kä ...
a good restaurant	**un buen restaurante?** o͞on bo͞o·en' restourän'te?
an inexpensive restaurant	**un restaurante barato?** o͞on restourän'te bärä'tō?
a typical restaurant	**un restaurante típico?** o͞on restourän'te tē'pēkō?
a bar	**un bar?** o͞on bär?
a saloon	**una cantina** o͞o'nä käntē'nä
a café	**una cafetería?** o͞o'nä käfeterē'ä?

INFO All Latin American cities have expensive restaurants which cater to the rich and to tourists. Check the prices on the menu posted outside. Moderately priced restaurants with good food can usually be found centered around the main **plaza** of a typical town. They usually offer a daily special, **la comida corrida**. Cafeteria type restaurants, often called **loncherías** or **comedores,** usually offer good food at reasonable prices. You will also find American fast food chains throughout Latin America, especially in the cities. There are many food stalls on the streets with tasty looking food, but caution is advised. Big cities have bars and nightclubs. Typical **cantinas**, saloons, are places for heavy drinking and are patronized by men only.

A table for …, please.	**Por favor, una mesa para … personas.** pōr fävōr', o͞o'nä me'sä pä'rä … persō'näs.
I'd like to reserve a table for … persons at … o'clock	**Quisiera reservar una mesa para … personas a las …** kēsye'rä reservär' o͞o'nä me'sä pä'rä … persō'näs ä läs …

INFO Occasionally a small restaurant might not have a printed menu. Look around for a signboard or you can ask 'What do you have today?' **¿Qué hay hoy?**

Do you have a highchair?	**¿Tienen una silla para el niño?** ¿tye'nen o͞o'nä sē'lyä pä'rä el nē'nyō?
Excuse me, where are the restrooms?	**Perdone, ¿dónde están los baños ⟨Sp: los servicios⟩?** perdō'ne, ¿dōn'de estän' lōs bä'nyōs ⟨Sp: lōs servē'syōs⟩?

! **Alli detrás.** älyē' deträs'. — In the back.

WAITER!

INFO Although you might hear people making a kind of hiss ('psst') to get the waiter's attention, you can just call for the waiter '**Mesero**' or for the waitress '**Señorita.**'

May I see a menu please?	**Me trae la carta, por favor.** me trä'e lä kär'tä, pōr fävōr.

I'd like something to eat. — **Quisiera comer algo.** kēsye'rä kōmer' äl'gō.

I'd just like a snack. — **Sólo quiero picar un poco.** sō'lō kye'rō pēkär' o͞on pō'kō.

INFO Breakfast in Latin America and Spain is not as large as in the United States. It usually consists of coffee, tea or hot chocolate and some sort of bread or pastry. Toast is **pan tostado** 〈**Sp: una tostada**〉, rolls are **bolillos** or **panecillos.** In Mexico, **pan dulce**, a type of sweet bread, might be served in the mornng.

Are you still serving meals? — **¿Se puede comer?** ¿se po͞o·e'de kōmer'?

? **¿Qué desean?** ¿ke dese'än? — What would you like to eat?

? **¿Qué quiere de *primero*/ *segundo*?** ¿ke kye're de *prēme'rō* / *sego͞on'dō*? — What would you like as a *first*/ *second* course?

I'd like a portion of… — **Quisiera una porción 〈Sp: una ración〉 de …** kēsye'rä o͞o'nä pōrsyōn' 〈Sp: o͞o'nä räsyōn'〉 de…

Do you have ...? — **¿Tienen ...?** ¿tye'nen…?

Do you have any regional specialties? — **¿Cuáles son los platos típicos de la región?** ¿ko͞o·ä'les sōn lōs plä'tōs tē'pēkōs de lä rehē·ōn'?

What would you recommend?	**¿Qué me recomienda?** ¿ke me rekōmyen'dä?

! **Le recomiendo …** le rekōmyen'dō … — I can recommend…

Do you serve…	**¿Tienen…** ¿tye'nen …
vegetarian dishes?	**comida vegetariana?** kōmē'dä ve<u>h</u>etäryä'nä?
diabetic meals?	**platos especiales para diabéticos?** plä'tōs espesyä'les pä'rä dē·äbe'tēkōs?
dietary meals?	**comida de régimen?** kōmē'dä de re'<u>h</u>ēmen?
Does it have …? I'm not allowed to eat any.	**¿Lleva este plato …? No lo puedo comer.** ¿lye'vä es'te plä'tō …? no lo pōō·e'dō kōmer'.

? **¿Tomará** ***primer plato/postre*****?** ¿tōmärä' *prēmer' plä'tō/pōs'tre*? — Would you care for *an appetizer/some dessert*?

No, thank you, I don't care for *an appetizer/any dessert.*	**No voy a tomar** ***primer plato/postre.*** **Gracias.** nō voi ä tōmär' *prēmer' plä'tō/pōs'tre.* grä'syäs.
Could I have … instead of…?	**¿Podría traerme … en lugar de …?** ¿pōdrē'ä trä·er'me … en lōōgär' de …?

? **¿Cómo desea el bistec?** ¿kō'mō dese'ä el bēstek'? — How would you like your steak?

4

Rare.	**Casi crudo ⟨Sp: Poco hecho⟩.** kä'sē kro͞o'dō ⟨Sp: pō'kō e'tshō⟩.
Medium.	**Medio cocido ⟨Sp: hecho⟩.** me'dyō kōsē'dō ⟨Sp: e'tshō⟩.
Well-done.	**Bien cocido ⟨Sp: hecho⟩.** byen' kōsē'dō ⟨Sp: e'tshō⟩.
Could you bring me …, please?	**Por favor, tráigame …** pōr fävōr', trī'gäme …

INFO If you want to eat just a little, try a sandwich. They are made with rolls and filled with ham, chicken, cheese, beans, etc.

? **¿Qué desea tomar ⟨Sp: beber⟩?** ¿ke dese'ä tōmär ⟨Sp: beber'⟩? — What would you like to drink?

I'd like …, please.	**Quisiera …** kēsye'rä.
red wine	**un tinto.** o͞on tēn'tō.
a beer	**una cerveza.** o͞o'nä serve'sä.
one liter/half a liter of white wine	***un/medio*** **litro de vino blanco.** *o͞on/me'dyō* lē'trō de vē'nō bläng'kō.
a pitcher of water	**una jarra de agua.** o͞o'nö h̲ä'rä de ä'go͞o·ä.
a quarter of a liter of rosé	**un cuarto de litro de rosado.** øn ko͞o·är'tō de lē'trō de rōsä'dō.
a cup of coffee	**un café.** o͞on käfe'.

INFO If you order **café con leche** you'll get half espresso and half steaming milk. If you want filter coffee ask for **café estilo americano**. Instant coffee, very widespread, is known by the brand name **Nescafé**. Black tea, **té negro,** might be difficult to find in smaller towns. **Chocolate**, hot chocolate, is a very popular drink.

Do you have a house wine?	**¿Tienen un vino de la casa?** ¿tye'nen o͞on vē'nō de lä kä'sä?

COMPLAINTS

Excuse me, I didn't order this. I wanted …	**Disculpe, pero no he pedido esto. Yo quería …** dēsko͞ol'pe, pe'rō nō e pedē'dō es'tō. yō kerē'ä …
We asked for …	**Todavía *falta / faltan* …** to͞odävē'ä *fäl' tä / fäl' tän* …
The meat hasn't been cooked enough.	**La carne no ha sido bien cocida ⟨Sp: hecha⟩.** lä kär'ne nō ä sēē'dō byen' kōsē'dä ⟨Sp: e'tshä⟩.
Could you take it back, please?	**Por favor, lléveselo.** pōr fävōr', lye'veselō.

THE CHECK, PLEASE!

Could I have the check, please?	**La cuenta, por favor.** lä ko͞oen'tä, pōr fävōr'.
I'd like a receipt.	**Por favor, quisiera un recibo.** pōr fävōr', kesye'rä o͞on resēē'bō.

I'd like to pay for your meal.

Déjeme que *le/te* invite.
de'h̲eme ke *le/te* ēnvē'te.

We'd like separate checks, please.

Queremos pagar por separado.
kere'mōs pägär' pōr sepärä'dō.

INFO When dining in a group where each person wants to pay individually, it is customary to have one person pay the entire bill, get a receipt, **recibo**, and settle up later.

All together, please.

Por favor, todo junto.
pōr fävōr', tō'dō h̲o͞on'tō.

? **¿Le ha gustado?**
¿le ä go͞ostä'dō?

Did you enjoy your meal?

It was very nice, thank you.

Estaba todo muy bueno, gracias.
estä'bä tō'dō mo͞o'ē bo͞o·e'nō, grä'syäs.

I don't think this is correct.

Creo que aquí hay un error.
kre'ō ke äkē' ī o͞on erōr'.

Could we look over the check?

Por favor, ¿podríamos revisar juntos la cuenta? pōr fävōr', ¿pōdrē'ämōs revēsär' h̲o͞on'tōs lä ko͞o·en'tä?

We didn't order this.

No hemos pedido esto.
nō e'mōs pedē'dō es'tō.

Thank you, this is for you.

Muchas gracias, esto es para usted.
mo͞o'tshäs grä'syäs, e'stō es pä'rä o͞oste'.

DINING WITH FRIENDS

Enjoy your meal!	**¡Que aproveche!** ¡ke äprōve'tshe!
Cheers!	**¡Salud!** ¡sälo͞od'!
? **¿*Le*/*Te* gusta?** ¿*le*/*te* go͞os'tä?	How are you enjoying your meal?
It's very good, thank you.	**Muy bueno, gracias.** mo͞o'ē bo͞o·e'nō, grä'syäs.
? **¿Un poco más de ...?** ¿o͞on pō'kō mäs de ...?	Would you like some more ...?
Yes, please.	**Sí, por favor.** sē, pōr fävōr'.
No thank you, I'm full.	**No gracias, ya he comido bastante.** nō grä'syäs, yä e kōmē'dō bästän'te.
What's this?	**¿Qué es esto?** ¿ke es es'tō?
Would you pass me the ..., please?	**¿*Podría*/*Podrías* pasarme ...?** ¿*pōdrē'ä*/*pōdrē'äs* päsär'me ...?
Do you mind if I smoke?	**¿*Le*/*Te* molesta que fume?** ¿*le*/*te* mōles'tä ke fo͞o'me?
Thank you for the invitation.	**Muchas gracias por la invitación.** mo͞o'tshäs grä'syäs pōr lä ēnvētäsyōn'.
It was delicious.	**Estaba exquisito.** estä'bä ekskēsē'tō.

➡ *See also: Please; Thank you (p. 26)*

4

alcohol	**el alcohol** el älkō·ōl
appetizer	**el aperitivo** el äperētē'vō
bar	**el bar** el bär
beer	**la cerveza** lä serve'sä
beverage menu	**la lista de bebidas** lä lē'stä de bebē'däs
black coffee	**el café solo** el käfe' sō'lō
bottle	**la botella** lä bōte'lyä
bottle opener	**el destapador ⟨Sp: abridor⟩** el destäpädōr' ⟨Sp: äbrēdōr'⟩
bread	**el pan** el pän
breakfast	**el desayuno** el desäyo͞o'nō
to bring	**traer** trä·er'
butter	**la manteca ⟨Sp: la mantequilla⟩** lä mänte'kä ⟨Sp: lä mäntekē'lyä⟩
carafe	**la jarra** lä ẖä'rä
chamomile tea	**la manzanilla** lä mänsänē'lyä
cheese	**el queso** el ke'sō
chocolate	**el chocolate** el tshōkōlä'te
coffee	**el café** el käfe'
coffee with milk	**el café con leche** el käfe' kōn le'tshe
cold	**frío** frē'ō
corkscrew	**el sacacorchos** el säkäkōr'tshōs
course	**el plato** el plä'tō
cream	**la crema ⟨Sp: la nata⟩** lä kre'mä ⟨Sp. lä nä'tä⟩
cup	**la taza** lä tä'sä
cutlery	**los cubiertos** lōs ko͞obyer'tōs

decaf **el café descafeinado** el käfe' deskäfe·ēnä'dō
dessert **el postre** el pōs'tre
diabetic **el diabético** el dē·äbe'tēkō
dinner **la cena** lä se'nä
dish of the day **el plato del día** el plä'tō del dē'ä
drink **la bebida** lä bebē'dä
to drink **tomar** ⟨**Sp: beber**⟩ tōmär' ⟨Sp: beber'⟩
eat **comer** kōmer'
egg **el huevo** el o͞o·e'vō
filter coffee **el café de filtro** el käfe' de fēl'trō
fish **el pescado** el peskä'dō
food **la comida** lä kōmē'dä
fork **el tenedor** el tenedōr'
free **libre** lē'bre
fresh **fresco** fres'kō
fried egg **el huevo frito** el o͞o·e'vō frē'tō
garlic **el ajo** el ä'h̲ō
glass *(drinking)* **el vaso** el vä'sō
ham **el jamón** el h̲ämōn'
hard **duro** do͞o'rō
high chair **la silla para niños** lä sē'lyä pä'rä ne'nyōs
honey **la miel** lä myel'
hot **caliente** kälyen'te
to be hungry **tener hambre** tener' äm'bre
ice cube **el cubito de hielo** el ko͞obē'tō de ye'lō
jam **la mermelada** lä mermelä'dä

4

knife	**el cuchillo** el ko͞otshē'lyō
lettuce	**la lechuga** lä letsho͞o'gä
lunch	**el almuerzo** el älmo͞o·er'sō
main course	**el segundo plato** el sego͞on'dō plä'tō
meat	**la carne** lä kär'ne
menu	**la carta** lä kär'tä
milk	**la leche** lä le'tshe
mineral water	**el agua mineral** el ä'go͞o·ä mēneräl'
carbonated –	**el agua mineral con gas** el ä'go͞o·ä mēneräl' kōn gäs
non-carbonated –	**el agua mineral sin gas** el ä'go͞o·ä mēneräl' sēn gäs
mint	**la menta** lä men'tä
mushrooms	**los champiñones** lōs tshämpēnyō'nes
mustard	**la mostaza** lä mōstä'sä
napkin	**la servilleta** lä servēlye'tä
non-alcoholic	**sin alcohol** sēn älkō·ōl'
oil	**el aceite** el äse'ēte
olive oil	**el aceite de oliva** el äse'ēte de ōlē'vä
olives	**las aceitunas** läs äse'ēto͞o'näs
one check	**pagar todo junto** pägär' tō'dō h̲o͞on'tō
to order	**pedir** pedēr'
pastry	**los pasteles** ***m/pl*** läs päste'les
to pay	**pagar** pägär
to pay for *someone's* meal	**invitar a** ēnvētär' ä
pepper	**la pimienta** lä pēmyen'tä
piece	**el trozo** el trō'sō

plate	**el plato** el plä'tō
portion	**la porción ⟨Sp: la ración⟩** lä pōrsyōn' ⟨Sp: lä räsyōn'⟩
pound cake	**el bizcocho** el bēskō'tshō
to recommend	**recomendar** rekōmendär'
to reserve	**reservar** reservär'
rest room	**los baños** ***m/pl*** **⟨Sp: servicios** ***m/pl*****⟩** lōs bä'nyōs ⟨Sp: servē'syōs⟩
roll	**el bolillo ⟨Sp: panecillo⟩** el bōlēl'yō ⟨Sp: pänesēl'yō⟩
salad	**la ensalada** lä ensä'lä'dä
salt	**la sal** lä säl
sandwich	**el sandwich ⟨Sp: bocadillo⟩** el sänvētsh' ⟨Sp: bōkädēl'yō⟩
sauce	**la salsa** lä säl'sä
scrambled egg	**el huevo revuelto** el o͞o·e'vō revo͞o·el'tō
separate checks	**pagar por separado** pägär' pōr sepärä'dō
soup	**la sopa** lä sō'pä
spicy	**picante** pēkän'te
spoon	**la cuchara** lä ko͞otshä'rä
straw	**la pajita** lä päh̲ē'h̲ä
sugar	**el azúcar** el äs̲o͞o'kär
sweet	**dulce** do͞ol'se
table	**la mesa** lä me'sä
table setting	**el cubierto** el ko͞obyer'tō
tea	**el té** el te
teaspoon	**la cucharilla** lä ko͞otshärē'lyä
to be thirsty	**tener sed** tener' sed

to try	**probar** prōbär'
vegetables	**las verduras** läs verdo͞o'räs
vegetarian	**vegetariano** ve_hetäryä'nō
water	**el agua** el ä'go͞o·ä
water (carbonated)	**el agua mineral con gas** el ä'go͞o·ä mēneräl' kōn gäs
water (non-carbonated)	**el agua mineral sin gas** el ä'go͞o·ä mēneräl' sēn gäs
white bread	**el pan blanco** el pän bläng'kō
whole grain bread	**el pan integral** el pän ēntegräl'
wine	**el vino** el vē'nō

See also: Food and Drink (p. 146)

Sightseeing

TOURIST INFORMATION

May I have ...	**Quisiera ...** kēsye'rä...
a list of hotels?	**una lista de hoteles.** o͞o'nä lēs'tä de ōte'les.
a map of the surrounding area?	**un mapa de los alrededores.** o͞on mä'pä de lōs älrededō'res.
a map of the town?	**un plano de la ciudad.** o͞on plä'nō de lä syo͞odäd'.
a map of the subway?	**un mapa del metro.** o͞on mä'pä del me'trō.
a current-events guide?	**un programa de actividades.** o͞on prōgrä'mä de äktēvēdä'des.

INFO **Oficinas de Información y Turismo** (Tourist Information Bureaus) provide information on sights and accommodations etc. They are found in every large town and in most villages, too.

Could you reserve a hotel room for me?	**¿Puede reservarme un cuarto ⟨Sp: una habitación⟩?** ¿po͞o·e'de reservär'me o͞on ko͞o·är'tō ⟨Sp: o͞o'nä äbētäsyōn'⟩?
Are there sightseeing tours?	**¿Organizan circuitos turísticos?** ¿ōrgänē'sän sērko͞o·ē'tōs to͞orēs'tēkōs?
How much is the sightseeing tour?	**¿Cuánto cuesta el circuito turístico?** ¿ko͞o·än'tō ko͞o·es'tä el sērko͞o·ē'tō to͞orēs'tēkō?

How long is the sightseeing tour?	**¿Cuánto dura el circuito turístico?** ¿kōō·än'tō dōō'rä el sērkōō·ē'tō tōōrēs'tēkō?
One ticket/ two tickets for the sightseeing tour, please	**Por favor, *un boleto/ dos boletos* ⟨Sp: billete(s)⟩ para el circuito turístico.** pōr fävōr', *ōōn bōle'tō/ dōs bōle'tōs* ⟨Sp: belye'te(s)⟩ pä'rä el sērkōō·ē'tō tōōrēs'tēkō.
I'd like to visit…	**Quisiera visitar…** kēsye'rä vēsētär'…
One ticket/ two tickets for tomorrow's tour, please.	**Por favor, *una plaza/ dos plazas* para la excursión mañana.** pōr fävōr', *ōō'nä plä'sä/ dōs plä'säs* pä'rä lä ekskōōrsyōn' mänyä'nä.
When/ Where do we meet?	**¿*Cuándo/ Dónde* nos encontramos?** ¿*kōō·än'dō/ dōn'de* nōs enkōnträ'mōs?
Are we also going to see…?	**¿Vamos a visitar… también?** ¿vä'mōs ä vēsētär'… tämbyen'?
When do we start?	**¿Cuándo salimos?** ¿kōō·än'dō sälēmōs?
When do we get back?	**¿Cuándo volvemos?** ¿kōō·än'dō vōlve'mōs?

➡ *Hotel reservation: Accommodations (p. 36)*

➡ *Public transportation: Bus, Subway, Taxi (p. 87)*

5

SIGHTSEEING, EXCURSIONS

When/How long is … open?	***¿Cuándo/Hasta cuándo* está ♂ abierto/♀ abierta …?** *¿'koo͞·än'do/äs'tä koo͞·än'do estä'* ♂ äbyer'tō/♀ äbyer'tä …?

INFO Check at your hotel or at the tourist office on the opening times of museums, exhibitions and other places you want to visit. Some museums may close at lunchtime, others may be closed for renovation, most may be closed on public holidays.

What's the admission charge?	**¿Cuánto cuesta la entrada?** ¿koo͞·än'tō koo͞·es'tä lä enträ'dä?
How much does the guided tour cost?	**¿Cuánto cuesta la visita con guía?** ¿koo͞·än'tō koo͞·es'tä lä vēsē'tä kōn gē'ä?
Is there a discount for….	**¿Hay precios especiales para …** ¿ī pre'syōs espesyä'les pä'rä …
groups?	**grupos?** groo͞'pōs?
children?	**niños?** nē'nyōs?
senior citizens?	**pensionistas?** pensyōnēs'täs?
students?	**estudiantes?** estoo͞dyän'tes?

? **¿Tiene *una tarjeta* ⟨*Sp: un carnet*⟩ *de identidad*/*un pasaporte*?** ¿tye'ne oo͞'nä tär<u>he</u>'tä ⟨Sp: kärnet'⟩ de ēdentēdäd/päsäpōr'te? — Do you have your *ID*/*passport* with you?

Are there guided tours in English?	**¿Hay visitas con guía en inglés?** ¿ī vēsē'täs kōn gē'ä en ēng·gles'?
When does the guided tour begin?	**¿Cuándo comienza la visita guiada?** ¿ko͞o·än'dō kōmyen'sä lä vēsē'tä gē·ä'dä?
Two tickets, please.	**Dos boletos (Sp: entradas), por favor.** dōs bōle'tōs (Sp: enträ'däs), pōr fävōr'.
Two adults and two children, please.	**Dos adultos y dos niños, por favor.** dōs ädo͞ol'tōs ē dōs nē'nyōs, pōr fävōr'.
Is videotaping allowed?	**¿Se puede grabar en vídeo?** ¿se po͞o·e'de gräbär' en vēde'ō?
Is photography allowed?	**¿Se puede sacar fotos?** ¿se po͞o·e'de säkär' fō'tōs?
What *building/ monument* is that?	**¿Qué *edificio/ monumento* es ése?** ¿ke *edēfē'syō/ mōno͞omen'tō* es e'se?
Do you have a *catalogue/ guide*?	**¿Tienen *un catálogo/ una guía*?** ¿tye'nen *o͞on kätä'lōgō/ o͞o'nä gē'ä*?
Do you have this picture on a	**¿Tienen este cuadro en …** ¿tye'nen es'te ko͞o·ä'drō en …
slide?	**díapositiva?** dē·äpōsētē'vä?
poster?	**póster?** pōs'ter?
post card?	**tarjeta postal?** tärhe'tä pōstäl'?

abbey	**la abadía** lä äbädē'ä
altar	**el altar** el ältär'
amphitheater	**el anfiteatro** el änfēte·ä'trō
antiquity	**la antigüedad** lä äntēgōō·edäd'
aqueduct	**el acueducto** el äkōō·edōōk'tō
arch	**el arco** el är'kō
archeology	**la arqueología** lä ärkē·ōlō<u>h</u>ē'ä
architect	**el arquitecto** el ärkētek'tō
architecture	**la arquitectura** lä ärkētektōō'rä
art	**el arte** el är'te
artist	**el artista** el ärtēs'tä
Aztec	**azteca** äste'kä
Baroque	**el barroco** el bärō'kō
basilica	**la basílica** lä bäsē'lekä
bell	**la campana** lä kämpä'nä
botanical garden(s)	**el jardín botánico** el <u>h</u>ärdēn' bōtä'nēkō
bridge	**el puente** el pōō·en'te
brochure	**el folleto** el fōlye'tō
bullring	**la plaza de toros** lä plä'sä de tō'rōs
bust	**el busto** el bōōs'tō
castle	**el castillo** el kästē'lyō
cathedral	**la catedral** lä kätedräl'
cave	**la cueva** lä kōō·e'vä
ceiling	**el techo** el te'tshō
cemetery	**el cementerio** el sementer'yō
century	**el siglo** el sē'glō
chapel	**la capilla** lä käpē'lyä

choir **el coro (de la iglesia)** el kō'rō (de lä ēgle'syä)
church **la iglesia** lä ēgle'syä
church tower **la torre de la iglesia** lä tō're de lä ēgle'syä
city hall **la alcaldía ⟨Sp: el ayuntamiento⟩** lä älkäldē'ä ⟨Sp: el äyōōntämyen'tō⟩
cloister **el claustro** el klou'strō
closed **cerrado** serä'dō
coat-of-arms **el escudo** el eskōō'dō
collection **la colección** lä kōleksyōn'
colonial **colonial** kōlōnyäl'
Columbus **Colón** kōlōn'
column **la columna** lä kōlōōm'nä
conquistador **el conquistador** el kōnkēstädōr'
Corinthian **corintio** kōrēn'tyō
cross **la cruz** lä krōōs
desert **el desierto** el desyer'tō
discoverer **el descubridor** el deskōōbrēdōr'
dome **la cúpula** lä kōō'pōōlä
Doric **dórico** dō'rēkō
downtown **el centro** el sen'trō
drawing **el dibujo** el debōō'hō
dry season **el tiempo de secas** el tyem'pō de se'käs
emperor **el emperador** el emperädōr'
empress **la emperatriz** lä emperätrēs'
epoch **la época** lä e'pōkä
excavations **las excavaciones *f/pl*** läs ekskäväsyō'nes

5

excursion	**la excursión** lä ekskōōrsyōn'
exhibition	**la exposición** lä ekspōsēsyōn'
façade	**la fachada** lä fätshä'dä
to film	**filmar** fēlmär'
forest	**el bosque** el bōs'ke
forest fire	**el incendio forestal** el ēnsen'dyō fōrestäl'
fort	**la fortaleza** lä fōrtäle'sä
fountain	**la fuente** lä fōō·en'te
fresco	**el fresco** el fres'kō
funicular railway	**el funicular** el fōōnēkōōlär'
garden	**el jardín** el härdēn'
gate	**la puerta** lä pōō·er'tä
gorge	**la garganta** lä gärgän'tä
Gothic	**el gótico** el gō'tēkō
grave	**el sepulcro** el sepōōl'krō
guided tour	**la visita guiada** lä vēsē'tä gē·ä'dä
harbor	**el puerto** el pōō·er'tō
Hispanic	**hispánico** ēspä'nēkō
history	**la historia** lä ēstōr'yä
house	**la casa** lä kä'sä
indigenous peoples	**la población indígena** lä pōbläsyōn' ēndē'henä
jai alai palace	**el frontón** el frōntōn'
king	**el rey** el re'ē
lake	**el lago** el lä'gō
landscape	**el paisaje** el pīsä'he
main entrance	**el portal** el pōrtäl'
marble	**el mármol** el mär'mōl

market	**el mercado**	el merkä'dō
mass	**la misa**	lä mē'sä
memorial	**el lugar conmemorativo**	el lo͞ogär' kōnmemōrätē'vō
Middle Ages	**la edad media**	lä edäd' me'dyä
modern	**moderno**	mōder'nō
monastery	**el monasterio**	el mōnäste'ryō
monument	**el monumento**	el mōno͞omen'tō
Moorish	**morisco**	mōrēs'kō
mosaic	**el mosaico**	el mōsī'kō
mosque	**la mezquita**	lä meskē'tä
mountain range	**la sierra**	lä sye'rä
mural	**la pintura mural**	lä pēnto͞o'rä mo͞oräl'
museum	**el museo**	el mo͞ose'ō
national park	**el parque nacional**	el pär'ke näsyōnäl'
nature preserve	**la reserva natural**	lä reser'vä näto͞oräl'
neighborhood	**el barrio**	el bär'yō
old	**antiguo**	äntē'go͞o·ō
old part of town	**el casco antiguo**	el käs'kō äntē'go͞o·ō
open	**abierto**	äbyer'tō
opera	**la ópera**	lä ō'perä
Order	**la orden**	lä ōr'den
organ	**el órgano**	el ōr'gänō
original	**el original**	el ōrēhēnäl'
painter	**el pintor**	el pēntōr'
painting	**la pintura**	lä pēnto͞o'rä
palace	**el palacio**	el pälä'syō
park	**el parque**	el pär'ke
patio	**el patio**	el pä'tyō

5

pedestrian zone	**la zona peatonal** lä sō'nä pe·ätōnäl'
picture	**el cuadro** el ko͞o·ä'drō
pilgrim	**el peregrino** el peregrē'nō
portrait	**el retrato** el reträ'tō
post card	**la tarjeta postal** lä tär<u>h</u>e'tä pōstäl'
pottery	**la alfarería** lä älfärerē'ä
pre-Colombian	**precolombino** pre-kōlōmbē'nō
protection of monuments	**la conservación de monumentos** lä kōnserväsyōn' de mōno͞omen'tōs
pyramid	**la pirámide** lä pērä'mēde
queen	**la reina** lä re'ēnä
rain forest	**la pluviselva** lä plo͞ovēsel'vä
rainy season	**el tiempo de lluvias** el tyem'pō de lyo͞o'vyäs
ranch	**el rancho** el rän'tshō
to reconstruct	**reconstruir** rekōnstro͞o·ēr'
religion	**la religión** lä relē<u>h</u>ē·ōn'
Renaissance	**el Renacimiento** el renäsēmē·en'tō
to restore	**restaurar** restourär'
river	**el río** el rē'ō
Romanesque	**el románico** el rōmä'nēkō
romantic	**romántico** rōmän'tēkō
ruin	**la ruina** lä ro͞o·ē'nä
sandstone	**la arenisca** lä ärenēs'kä
sculptor	**el escultor** el esko͞oltōr'
sculpture	**la escultura** lä esko͞olto͞o'rä
sights	**los lugares de interés turístico** lōs lo͞ogä'res de ēnteres' to͞orēs'tēkō

sightseeing tour	**el circuito turístico** el sērkōōē'tō tōōrēs'tēkō
square	**la plaza** ⟨**Mex: el zócalo**⟩ lä pläsä ⟨Mex: el sō'kälō⟩
stalagmite and stalactite cave	**la cueva de estalagmitas y estalactitas** lä kōō·e'vä de estälägmē'täs ē estäläk-tē'täs
statue	**la estatua** lä estä'tōō·ä
street map	**el plano de la ciudad** el plä'nō de lä syōōdäd'
style	**el estilo** el estē'lō
synagogue	**la sinagoga** lä sēnägō'gä
to take photographs	**sacar una foto** säkär' ōō'nä fō'tō
temple	**el templo** el tem'plō
theater	**el teatro** el te·ä'trō
tourist guidebook	**el guía turístico** el gē'ä tōōrēs'tēkō
tourist information	**la información turística** lä ēnfōrmäsyōn' tōōrēs'tēkä
tower	**la torre** lä tō're
town	**la ciudad** lä syōōdäd'
town center	**el centro** el sen'trō
town wall	**la muralla** lä mōōrä'lyä
treasury	**la cámara del tesoro** lä kä'märä del tesō'rō
valley	**el valle** el vä'lye
vase	**el jarrón** el härōn'
to videotape	**grabar en vídeo** gräbär' en vee'deō
view	**la vista panorámica** lä vēs'tä pänōrä'mēkä

village	**el pueblo** el pōō'e'blō
visit	**la visita** lä vēsē'tä
to visit	**visitar** vēsētär'
volcano	**el volcán** el vōlkän'
wall	**el muro** el mōō'rō
window	**la ventana** lä ventä'nä
wine cellar	**la bodega** lä bōde'gä
wine tasting	**la degustación de vino** lä degōōstäsyōn' de vee'nō
wing *(of a building)*	**el ala** el ä'lä
wood carving	**la talla de madera** lä tä'lyä de mäde'rä
work of art	**la obra de arte** lä ō'brä de är'te
zone	**la zona** lä sō'nä
zoo	**el zoo** el sō'ō

Animals

bear	**el oso** el ō'sō
bee	**la abeja** lä äbe'h̲ä
bugs	**los bichos** lōs bē'tshōs
bull	**el toro** el tō'rō
cat	**el gato** el gä'tō
cow	**la vaca** lä vä'kä
dog	**el perro** el pe'rō
donkey	**el burro** el bōō'rō
eagle	**el águila** el ä'gēlä
frog	**la rana** lä rä'nä
goat	**la cabra** lä kä'brä
grasshopper	**el saltamontes** el sältämōn'tes
horse	**el caballo** el käbä'lyō

iguana	**la iguana** lä ēgo͞o·ä'nä
hare	**la liebre** lä lye'bre
lizard	**el lagartija** el lägärtē'ẖä
mouse	**el ratón** el rätōn'
mule	**el mulo** el mo͞o'lō
owl	**la lechuza ⟨Arg: el quitilipi⟩** lä letsho͞o'sä ⟨Arg: el kētēlē'pē⟩
parrot	**el loro** el lō'rō
pheasant	**el faisán** el fīsän'
scorpion	**el escorpión** el eskōrpyōn'
seagull	**la gaviota** lä gävyō'tä
snake	**la culebra (*nonpoisonous*); la víbora (*poisonous*)** lä ko͞ole'brä; lä vē'bōrä
spider	**la araña** läärän'yä
stork	**la cigüeña** lä sēgo͞o·e'nyä
tick	**la garrapata** lä gäräpä'tä
turtle	**la tortuga** lä tōrto͞o'gä
vulture	**el buitre** el bo͞o·ē'tre
wild cat	**el gato montés** el gä'tō mōntes'

Plants

acacia	**la acacia** lä äkä'syä
almond tree	**el almendro** el älmen'drō
aloe	**el áloe** el ä'lōe
apricot tree	**el damasco ⟨Mex: el chabacano, Sp: el albaricoquero⟩** el dämäs'kō ⟨Mex: el tshäbäkä'nō, Sp: el älbärēkōke'rō⟩
bougainvillea	**la buganvilla ⟨Sp: el buganvil⟩** lä bo͞ogänvē'lyä ⟨Sp: el bo͞ogänvēl'⟩

5

cacao palm	**el cacao** el käkä'ō
cedar	**el cedro** el sē'drō
century plant	**el agave** el ägä've
chestnut tree	**el castaño** el kästä'nyō
coffee bush	**el cafeto** el käfe'tō
cork tree	**el alcornoque** el älkōrnō'ke
cypress	**el ciprés** el cēpres'
eucalayptus	**el eucalipto** el e·o͞okälēp'tō
fig tree	**la higuera** lä ēge'rä
flower	**la flor** lä flōr
hazelnut bush	**el avellano** el ävelyä'nō
hyacinth	**el jacinto** el häsēn'tō
lavander	**la alhucema** lä älo͞ose'mä
lily	**la azucena** lä äso͞ose'nä
maple	**el arce** el är'se
oleander	**la adelfa** lä ädel'fä
olive tree	**el olivo** ōlē'vō
orange tree	**el naranjo** el närän'hō
orquid	**la orquidea** lä ōrkēde'ä
palm tree	**la palmera** lä pälme'rä
pine tree	**el pino** el pē'nō
tabacco plant	**el tabaco** el täbä'kō
thicket	**el matorral** el mätōräl'
tree	**el árbol** el är'bōl
walnut tree	**el nogal** el nōgäl'

Shopping

Where can I get…? **¿Dónde se puede conseguir…?** ¿dōn'de se pōō·e'de kōnsegēr'…?

INFO Latin America offers the visitor many opportunities to find interesting and unusual shopping items, especially typical arts and crafts. Unless you are shopping in a store with fixed prices, be sure to bargain. State run stores sell at set prices, and here you can be sure of authenticity and quality. Some popular souvenirs from Mexico include local handicrafts, instruments, hammocks, shell jewelry, embroidered clothing, papier-maché objects, and ceramics. There are also convincing imitations of pre-Colombian Mayan and Aztec artifacts (idols, **ídolos**); of course, it is illegal to purchase or export genuine artifacts.

? **¿Qué desea?** ¿ke dese'ä? — What would you like?

? **¿Ya *le*/ *la* atienden?** ¿yä *le*/*lä* atyen'den? — May I help you?

I'm just looking, thanks. — **Estoy mirando, gracias.** estōi' mērän'dō, grä'syäs.

I'm being helped, thanks. — **Ya me atienden, gracias.** yä me ätyen'den, grä'syäs.

I'd like… — **Quisiera…** kēsye'rä…

6

Could I have ..., please?	**Por favor, déme ...** pōr fävōr, de'me ...
a can of ...	**una lata de ...** ōō'nä lä'tä de ...
a bottle of ...	**una botella de ...** ōō'nä bōte'lyä de ...
a package of ...	**un paquete de ...** ōōn päke'te de ...

! **Lo siento, pero no nos queda ♂ *ningún*/ ♀ *ninguna* ...**
lō syen'tō, pe'rō nō nōs ke'dä ♂ *nēng·gōōn*/ ♀ *nēng·gōō'nä* ...
I'm sorry, we're out of ...

How much *is*/*are* ...?	**¿Cuánto *cuesta*/*cuestan* ...?** ¿kōō·än'tō *kōō·es'tä*/*kōō·es'tän* ...?
Please show me ...	**Por favor, enséñeme ...** pōr fävōr', ense'nyeme ...
I don't like it very much.	**No me gusta tanto.** no me gōō'stä tän'tō.
Could you show me something else?	**¿Puede enseñarme otra cosa?** ¿pōō·e'de ensenyär'me ō'trä kō'sä?
I'd like something cheaper.	**Quisiera algo más barato.** kēsye'rä äl'go mäs bärä'tō.
I'll have to think about it.	**Me lo tengo que pensar.** me lō teng'gō ke pensär'.
I like this. I'll take it.	**Me gusta. Me lo llevo.** me gōōs'tä. me lō lye'vō.

? **¿Desea otra cosa?** ¿dese'ä ō'trä kō'sä? — Will there be anything else?

That's all, thank you.	**Eso es todo, gracias.** e'sō es tō'dō, grä'syäs.
Can I pay with this credit card?	**¿Puedo pagar con esta tarjeta de crédito?** ¿po͞o·e'dō pägär' kōn es'tä tärh̲e'tä de kre'dētō?
Do you have a (plastic) bag?	**¿Tiene un bolso ⟨Sp: una bolsa⟩ (de plástico)?** ¿tye'ne o͞on bōl'sō ⟨Sp: o͞o'nä bōl'sä⟩ (de plä'stēcō)?
Could you giftwrap it, please?	**¿Puede empaquetármelo como regalo?** ¿po͞o·e'de empäketär'melō kō'mō regä'lō?
How much is it?	**¿Cuánto cuesta?** ¿ko͞o·än'tō ko͞o·es'tä?
Could I have a receipt, please?	**Por favor, ¿me puede dar un recibo?** pōr fävōr', ¿me po͞o·e'de där o͞on resē'bō?
It's broken. Can you fix it?	**Está dañado ⟨Sp: estropeado⟩. ¿Puede arreglarlo?** estä' dänyä'dō ⟨Sp: estrōpe·ä'dō⟩. ¿po͞o·e'de äreglär'lō?
When will it be ready?	**¿Cuándo estará listo?** ¿ko͞o·än'dō estärä' lēs'tō?
I'd like to *exchange/return* this.	**Quisiera *cambiar/devolver* esto.** kēsye'rä *kämbyär'/devōlver'* es'tō.

I'd like a refund, please.	**Quiero que me devuelva el dinero.** kye'rō ke me devo͞o·el'vä el dēne'rō.
I don't think this is the right change. I'm missing *(amount of money)*.	**Me ha devuelto** *(amount of money)* **de menos.** me ä devo͞o·el'tō … de me'nōs.

6

General Vocabulary

bargain	**la ganga** lä gäng'gä
to bargain	**regatear** regäte·är'
better	**mejor** meho̱r'
big	**grande** grän'de
bigger	**más grande** mäs grän'de
bottle	**la botella** lä bōte'lyä
to buy	**comprar** kōmprär'
can	**la lata** lä lä'tä
cheaper	**más barato** mäs bärä'tō
check	**el cheque** el tshe'ke
to cost	**costar** kōstär'
credit card	**la tarjeta de crédito** lä tärẖe'tä de kre'dētō
dark	**oscuro** ōsko͞o'rō
to exchange	**cambiar** kämbyär'
expensive	**caro** kä'rō
gift	**el regalo** el regä'lō
to give	**dar** där
to go shopping	**ir de compras** ēr de kōm'präs
heavy	**pesado** pesä'dō
light *(shade)*	**claro** klä'rō
light *(weight)*	**ligero** lēẖe'rō

money	**el dinero** el dēne'rō
more expensive	**más caro** mäs kä'rō
to pack	**empaquetar** empäketär'
package	**el paquete** el päke'te
plastic bag	**el bolso ⟨Sp: la bolsa⟩ de plástico** el bōl'sō ⟨Sp: lä bōl'sä⟩ de plä'stēcō
receipt	**el recibo** el resē'bō
to return	**devolver** devōlver'
round	**redondo** redōn'dō
sales	**las rebajas** ***f/pl*** läs rebä'h̲äs
self-service	**el autoservicio** el outōservē'syō
shop window	**el escaparate** el eskäpärä'te
to show	**enseñar** ensenyär'
small	**pequeño** peke'nyō
smaller	**más pequeño** mäs peke'nyō
soft	**blando** blän'dō
special offer	**la oferta especial** lä ōfer'tä espesyäl'
square	**cuadrado** ko͞o·ädrä'dō
too…	**demasiado…** demäsyä'dō…

INFO When entering stores, you might be requested to check your shopping bags at the door.

Clothing sizes differ from American sizes; try on or check carefully before you buy.

Sales are advertised by **oferta, ganga** or **rebajas.**

There are shopping malls, **centros comerciales**, in most Latin American cities.

Colors and Patterns

beige	**beige** be'ēsh
black	**negro** ne'grō
blue	**azul** äso͞ol'
brown	**marrón** märōn'
checked	**a cuadros** ä ko͞o·ä'drōs
colorful	**de colores** de kōlō'res
gray	**gris** grēs
green	**verde** ver'de
patterned	**estampado** estämpä'dō
pink	**rosa** rō'sä
purple	**morado** mōrä'dō
red	**rojo** rō'ẖō
solid-color	**de un color** de o͞on kōlōr'
striped	**a rayas** ä rä'yäs
violet	**lila** lē'lä
white	**blanco** bläng'kō
yellow	**amarillo** ämärē'lyō

Stores

antique shop	**la tienda de antigüedades** lä tyen'dä de äntēgo͞o·edä'des
bakery	**la panadería** lä pänäderē'ä
barber	**la peluquería** lä pelo͞okerē'ä
bookstore	**la librería** lä lēbrerē'ä
butcher's shop	**la carnicería** lä kärnēserē'ä
department store	**los grandes almacenes** ***m/pl*** los grän'des älmäse'nes

drugstore	**la farmacia** lä färmä'syä
dry cleaner's	**la limpieza en seco ⟨Sp: la tintorería⟩** lä lēmpē·e'sä en se'kō ⟨Sp: lä tēntōrerē'ä⟩
electrical appliance shop	**la tienda de electrodomésticos** lä tyen'dä de elektrōdōmes'tēkōs
fish market	**la pescadería** lä peskäderē'ä
florist	**la florería ⟨Sp: la floristería⟩** lä flōrerē'ä ⟨Sp: lä flōrēsterē'ä⟩
fruit market	**la frutería** lä froōterē'ä
hairdresser	**la peluquería** lä peloōkerē'ä
hardware store	**la ferretería** lä fereterē'ä
jewelry store	**la joyería** lä ho̱yerē'ä
leather shop	**la peletería** lä peleterē'ä
music store	**la tienda de discos** lä tyen'dä de dēs'kōs
newsstand	**el quiosco** el kē·ōs'kō
optician	**el óptico** el ōp'tēkō
perfume shop	**la perfumería** lä perfoōmerē'ä
photo (finishing) store	**el taller de fotografía** el tälyer' de fōtōgräfē'ä
shoe repair shop	**la zapatería** lä säpäterē'ä
shoemaker	**el zapatero** el säpäte'rō
souvenir shop	**la tienda de recuerdos** lä tyen'dä de rekoō·er'dōs
sporting goods store	**la tienda de artículos de deporte** lä tyen'dä de ärtē'koōlōs de depōr'te
stationery store	**la papelería** lä päpelerē'ä
supermarket	**el supermercado** el soōpermerkä'dō

tobacco shop	**el estanco** el estäng'kō
toy store	**la juguetería** lä h̲ōōgeterē'ä
vegetable market	**la verdulería** lä verdōōlerē'ä

FOOD

INFO There are two types of markets: permanent markets and temporary markets. Market day is **el día del marcado.** Indian markets are called **tianguis.** Always bargain in markets; it is considered a form of social contact. Carry enough change with you when shopping in markets. Weights are measured in kilo(gram)s (2.2 pounds) and liters (1.1 quarts).

What's that?	**¿Qué es eso?** ¿ke es e'sō?
Could I have…, please?	**Por favor, déme…** pōr fävōr', de'me…
100 grams of…	**cien gramos de…** syen' grä'mōs de…
one kilo of…	**un kilo de…** ōōn kē'lō de…
one/one half liter of…	**un/*medio* litro de…** *ōōn/me'dyō* lē'trō de…
half a kilo of…	**medio kilo de…** me'dyō kē'lō de…
a slice of…	**una rodaja de…** ōō'nä rōdä'h̲ä de…
a piece of…	**un trozo de…** ōōn trō'sō de…

? **¿Puede ser un poco más?** ¿pōō e'de ser ōōn pō'kō mäs? — Is a little more OK?

A little less, please. — **Un poco menos, por favor.**
o͞on pō'kō me'nōs, pōr fävōr'.

A little more, please. — **Un poco más, por favor.**
o͞on pō'kō mäs, pōr fävōr'.

May I try some of that, please? — **¿Podría probar un poco de eso?**
¿pōdrē'ä prōbär' o͞on pō'kō de e'sō?

Food and Drink

almonds	**las almendras** ***f/pl*** läs älmen'dräs
apple	**la manzana** lä mänsä'nä
apricot	**el damasco ⟨Mex: chabacano, Sp: el albaricoque⟩** el dämäs'kō ⟨Mex: el tshäbäkä'nō, Sp: el älbärekō'ke⟩
artichoke	**la alcachofa** lä älkätshō'fä
avocado	**el aguacate** el äg o͞oäkä'te
baby food	**el alimento infantil** el älēmen'tō ēnfäntēl'
banana	**la banana ⟨Sp: el plátano⟩** lä bänä'nä ⟨Sp: el plä'tänō⟩
beans	**los fríjoles** ***m/pl*** **⟨Sp: las judías** ***f/pl*****⟩** lōs frē'h̲ōles ⟨Sp: läs h̲o͞odē'äs⟩
beef	**la carne de res ⟨Sp: la carne de vaca⟩** lä kär'ne de res ⟨Sp: lä kär'ne de vä'kä⟩
beer	**la cerveza** lä serve'sä
bread	**el pan** el pän
breaded cutlet	**el escalope** el eskälō'pe
broccoli	**el brécol** el bre'kōl

butter	**la manteca ⟨Sp: la mantequilla⟩** lä mänte'kä ⟨Sp: lä mäntekē'lyä⟩
cake	**el pastel** el pästel'
candy	**los dulces *m/pl*** lōs do͞ol'ses
canned foods	**las conservas *f/pl*** läs kōnser'väs
carbonated	**con gas** kōn gäs
Cayenne pepper	**el pimentón** el pementōn'
cheese	**el queso** el ke'sō
cherries	**las cerezas *f/pl*** läs sere'säs
chick peas	**los garbanzos *m/pl*** lōs gärbän'sōs
chicken	**el pollo** el pō'lyō
chocolate	**el chocolate** el tshōkōlä'te
chop	**la chuleta** lä tsho͞ole'tä
cider	**la sidra** lä sē'drä
cocoa	**el cacao** el käkä'ō
coffee	**el café** el käfe'
cold cuts	**las carnes frías *f/pl* ⟨Sp: los fiambres *m/pl*⟩** lōs kär'nes frē'äs ⟨Sp: lōs fē·äm'bres⟩
cookies	**las galletas *f/pl*** läs gälye'täs
corn	**el maíz ⟨Chi: el choclo⟩** el mä·ēs' ⟨Ch: el tshō'klō⟩
cream	**la crema ⟨Sp: la nata⟩** lä kre'mä ⟨Sp: lä nä'tä⟩
cucumber	**el pepino** el pepē'nō
dates	**los dátiles *m/pl*** lōs dä'tēles
egg	**el huevo** el o͞o·e'vō
eggplant	**la berenjena** lä berenhe'nä
endive	**la endibia** lä endē'bē·ä

figs	**los higos** ***m/pl*** lōs ē'gōs
fish	**el pescado** el peskä'dō
fruit	**la fruta** lä frōō'tä
garlic	**el ajo** el ä'hō
goat's cheese	**el queso de cabra** el ke'sō de kä'brä
grapes	**las uvas** ***f/pl*** läs ōō'väs
green beans	**los ejotes** ***m/pl*** **⟨Sp: las judías verdes** ***f/pl*****⟩** lōs ehō'tes ⟨Sp: läs hōōdē'äs ver'des⟩
ham	**el jamón** el hämōn'
hamburger meat	**la carne molida ⟨Sp: picada⟩** lä kär'ne molē'dä ⟨Sp: pēkä'dä⟩
honey	**la miel** lä myel'
jam	**la mermelada** lä mermelä'dä
juice	**el jugo ⟨Sp: el zumo⟩** el hōō'gō ⟨Sp: el sōō'mō⟩
kiwi fruit	**el kiwi** el kē'vē
lamb	**la carne de cordero** lä kär'ne de kōrde'rō
leeks	**el puerro** el pōō·e'rō
lemon	**el limón** el lēmōn'
lettuce	**la lechuga** lä letshōō'gä
lowfat milk	**la leche desnatada** lä le'tshe desnätä'dä
margarine	**la margarina** lä märgärē'nä
meat	**la carne** lä kär'ne
melon	**el melón** el melōn'
milk	**la leche** lä le'tshe
mineral water	**el agua mineral** el ä'gōō·ä mēneräl'

non-alcoholic beer	**la cerveza sin alcohol** lä serve'sä sēn älkō·ōl'
non-carbonated	**sin gas** sēn gäs
nuts	**las nueces** ***f/pl*** läs no͞o·e'ses
oil	**el aceite** el äse'ēte
olive oil	**el aceite de oliva** el äse'ēte de ōlē'vä
olives	**las aceitunas** ***f/pl*** läs äse'eto͞o'näs
onion	**la cebolla** lä sebō'lyä
orange	**la naranja** lä närän'h̲ä
orange juice	**el jugo ⟨Sp: el zumo⟩ de naranja** el h̲o͞o'gō ⟨Sp: el so͞o'mō⟩ de närän'h̲ä
oysters	**los ostiones** ***m/pl*** **⟨Sp: las ostras⟩** ***f/pl*** lōs ostyō'nes ⟨Sp: läs ōs'träs⟩
pasta	**la pasta** lä päs'tä
peach	**el durazno ⟨Sp: el melocotón⟩** el do͞oräz'nō ⟨Sp: el melōkōtōn'⟩
peanuts	**los cacahuetes** ***m/pl*** lōs käkä·o͞o·e'tes
pear	**la pera** lä pe'rä
peas	**las arvejas** ***f/pl*** **⟨Méx: los chícharos** ***m/pl*****, Sp: los guisantes** ***m/pl*****⟩** läs ärve'h̲äs ⟨Mex: lōs tshē'tshärōs, Sp: los gēsän'tes⟩
pepper *(spice)*	**la pimienta** lä pēmyen'tä
pepper *(vegetable)*	**el pimiento** el pēmyen'tō
pickles	**los pepinillos en vinagre** ***m/pl*** lōs pepēnē'lyōs en vēnä'gre
pineapple	**el ananás ⟨Sp: la piña⟩** el änänäs' ⟨Sp: lä pē'nyä⟩

pork	**la carne de puerco** ⟨**Sp: de cerdo**⟩ lä kär'ne de po͞o·er'kō ⟨Sp: de ser'dō⟩
potatoes	**las papas** ***f/pl*** ⟨**Sp: las patatas** ***f/pl***⟩ läs pä'päs ⟨Sp: läs pätä'täs⟩
poultry	**las aves** ***f/pl*** läs ä'ves
pound cake	**el bizcocho** el bēskō'tshō
quince	**el membrillo** el membrē'lyō
raspberries	**las frambuesas** ***f/pl*** läs främbo͞o·e'säs
red chile pepper	**la guindilla** lä gēndē'lyä
red wine	**el vino tinto** e vē'nō tēn'tō
rice	**el arroz** el ärōs'
roll	**el bolillo** ⟨**Sp: el panecillo**⟩ el bōlē'lyo ⟨Sp: el pänesē'lyō⟩
salad	**la ensalada** lä ensälä'dä
salt	**la sal** lä säl
sandwich meats	**los embutidos** lōs embo͞otē'dōs
sausages	**las salchichas** ***f/pl*** läs sältshē'tshäs
sheep cheese	**el queso de oveja** el ke'sō de ōve'h̲ä
smoked ham	**el jamón curado** el hämōn' ko͞orä'dō
soft drink	**el refresco** el refres'kō
strawberries	**las fresas** ***f/pl*** ⟨**Arg, Par, Pe: las frutillas** ***f/pl***⟩ läs fre'säs ⟨Arg, Par, Pe: läs fro͞otē'lyäs⟩
sugar	**el azúcar** el äso͞o'kär
sweetener	**la sacarina** lä säkärē'nä
tea	**el té** el te
tomato	**el tomate** el tōmä'te
tuna	**el atún** el äto͞on'

veal	**la carne de res ⟨Sp: la carne de ternera⟩** lä kär'ne de res ⟨Sp: lä kär'ne de terne'rä⟩
vegetables	**la verdura** lä verdo͞o'rä
vinegar	**el vinagre** el vēnä'gre
watermelon	**la sandía** lä sändē'ä
white bread	**el pan blanco** el pän bläng'kō
white wine	**el vino blanco** el vē'no bläng'kō
wine	**el vino** el vē'nō
yogurt	**el yogur** el yōgo͞or'
zucchini	**el calabacín** el käläbäsēn'

SOUVENIRS

I'd like a souvenir. — **Quisiera un recuerdo.** kēsye'rä o͞on reko͞o·er'dō.

What's typical of this area? — **¿Qué hay típico en esta zona?** ¿ke ī tē'pēkō en es'tä sō'nä?

Is this handmade? — **¿Está hecho a mano?** ¿estä' e'tshō ä mä'nō?

Is this *old/genuine*? — **¿Es *antiguo/auténtico*?** ¿es *äntē'go͞o·ō/outen'tēkō*?

Souvenirs

antique	**antiguo** äntē'go͞o·ō
bag *(large)*	**el saco** el sä'kō
belt	**el cinturón** el sēnto͞orōn'

blanket	**la cobija ⟨Sp: la manta⟩** lä kōbē'ẖä ⟨Sp: lä män'tä⟩
castanets	**las castañuelas *f/pl*** läs kästänyo͞o·e'läs
embroidered	**bordado** bōrdä'dō
fan	**el abanico** el äbänē'kō
genuine	**auténtico** outen'tēkō
hammock	**la hamaca** lä ẖämä'kä
hand-carved	**tallado a mano** tälyä'dō ä mä'nō
handicrafts	**la artesanía** lä ärtesänē'ä
jewelry	**las joyas *f/pl*** läs ẖō'yäs
leather	**la piel** lä pyel'
mantilla *(lace head covering)*	**la mantilla** lä mäntē'lyä
old	**antiguo** äntē'go͞o·ō
pitcher	**la jarra** lä ẖä'rä
pottery	**la cerámica** lä serä'mēkä
pottery shop	**la alfarería** lä älfärerē'ä
souvenir	**el recuerdo** el reko͞o·er'dō
typical	**típico** tē'pēkō

CLOTHES AND DRY CLEANERS

I'm looking for… — **Estoy buscando…** estoi' bo͞oskän'dō…

? **¿Qué talla tiene usted?** ¿ke tä'lyä tye'ne o͞oste'? — What size do you take?

I'm size… — **Tengo la talla…** teng'gō lä tä'lyä…

Do you have this in another *size*/*color*? **¿Tienen este modelo en *otra talla*/ *otro color*?** ¿tye'nen es'te mōde'lō en *ō'trä tä'lyä*/*ō'trō kōlōr'*?

See also: word list Colors and Patterns (p. 143)

May I try this on? **¿Puedo probármelo?** ¿pōō·c'dō prōbär'melō?

Do you have a mirror? **¿Tienen un espejo?** ¿tye'nen ōōn espe'hō?

What kind of material is this? **¿De qué material es?** ¿de ke mäterē·äl' es?

It doesn't fit. **No me queda bien.** nō me ke'dä byen'.

This is too *big*/*small*. **Me queda *grande*/*pequeño*.** me ke'dä *grän'de*/*peke'nyō*.

See also: word list General Vocabulary (p. 141)

This fits well. **Me queda bien.** me ke'dä byen'.

I'd like this dry-cleaned, please. **Por favor, ¿me puede limpiar esto en seco?** pōr fävōr', ¿me pōō·e'de lēmpēär' es'tō en se'kō?

Could you remove this stain? **¿Podría quitar esta mancha?** ¿pōdrē'ä kētär' es'tä män'tshä?

Clothes and Dry Cleaner's

baby clothes **la ropa infantil** lä rō'pä ēnfäntēl'

bathrobe	**la bata de baño ⟨Sp: el albornoz⟩** lä bä'tä de bä'nyō ⟨Sp: el älbōrnōs'⟩
belt	**el cinturón** el sēnto͞orōn'
blouse	**la blusa** lä blo͞o'sä
bra	**el brasier ⟨Sp: el sujetador⟩** el bräsyer' ⟨Sp: el so͞oh̲etädōr'⟩
coat	**el sobretodo ⟨Sp: el abrigo⟩** el sōbretō'dō ⟨Sp: el äbrē'gō⟩
color	**el color** el kōlōr'
cotton	**el algodón** el älgōdōn'
dress	**el vestido** el vestē'dō
to dry clean	**limpiar en seco** lēmpyär' en se'kō
to fit	**quedar bien** kedär' byen'
gloves	**los guantes** ***m/pl*** lōs go͞o·än'tes
hat	**el sombrero** el sōmbre'rō
jacket	**la chaqueta** lä tshäke'tä
jeans	**el pantalón vaquero** el päntälōn' väke'rō
leather	**el cuero** el ko͞o·e'rō
lined	**forrado** fōrä'dō
linen	**el lino** el lē'nō
long	**largo** lär'gō
long sleeves	**las mangas largas** ***f/pl*** läs mäng'gäs lär'gäs
nightgown	**la camisa de dormir ⟨Sp: el camisón⟩** lä kämē'sä de dōrmēr' ⟨Sp: el kämēsōn'⟩
outfit	**el conjunto** el kōnh̲o͞on'tō
pajamas	**el pijama** el pēh̲ä'mä
pants	**el pantalón** el päntälōn'

pantyhose	**el panty ⟨Mex: las pantimedias *f/pl*, Arg: el can-can⟩** el pän'tē ⟨Mex: läs päntēme'dyäs, Arg: el kän-kän'⟩
parka	**el anorak** el änōräk'
raincoat	**el impermeable** el ēmperme·äb'le
scarf	**la bufanda** lä bo͞ofän'dä
shirt	**la camisa** lä kämē'sä
short	**corto** kōr'tō
shorts	**el pantalón corto** el päntälōn' kōr'tō
silk	**la seda** lä se'dä
size	**la talla** lä tä'lyä
skirt	**la falda** lä fäl'dä
sleeve	**la manga** lä mäng'gä
sports clothes	**la ropa deportiva** lä rō'pä depōrtē'vä
socks	**las medias *f/pl* ⟨Sp: los calcetines *m/pl*⟩** läs me'dyäs ⟨Sp: lōs kälsetē'nes⟩
sports coat	**el saco ⟨Sp: la americana⟩** el sä'kō ⟨Sp: lä ämerēkä'nä⟩
stockings	**las medias *f/pl*** läs me'dyäs
suit	**el traje** el trä'h̲e
sunhat	**el sombrero para el sol** el sōmbre'rō pä'rä el sōl
sweater	**el suéter ⟨Sp: el jersey⟩** el so͞o·e'ter ⟨Sp: el h̲er'sē⟩
sweatsuit	**el chandal** el tshän'däl
tie	**la corbata** lä kōrbä'tä
to try on	**probarse** prōbär'se
underpants *(men's)*	**los calzoncillos ⟨Sp: el slip⟩** lōs kälsōnsē'lyōs ⟨Sp: el slēp⟩

underpants *(women's)*	**las pantaletas *f/pl*** ⟨**Sp: las bragas *f/pl***⟩ läs päntäle'täs ⟨Sp: läs brä'gäs⟩
undershirt	**la camiseta** lä kämēse'tä
vest	**el chaleco** el tshäle'kō
wool	**la lana** lä lä'nä

SHOES

I'd like a pair of… — **Quiero un par de…** kye'rō o͞on pär de…

? **¿Qué número lleva?** ¿ke no͞o'merō lye'vä? — What size do you take?

My size is… — **Llevo el número…** lye'vō el no͞o'merō…

The heel is too *high*/*low*. — **El tacón es muy *alto*/*bajo*.** el täkōn' es mo͞o'ē *äl'tō*/*bä'ẖō*.

They are too *big*/*small*. — **Me están muy *grandes*/*pequeños*.** me estän' mo͞o'ē *grän'des*/*peke'nyōs*.

They're too tight around here. — **Me aprietan aquí.** me aprē·e'tän äkē'.

Please fix the *heels*/*soles*. — **Por favor, arregle *los tacones*/*las suelas*.** pōr fävōr', äre'gle *lōs täkō'nes*/*läs so͞o·e'läs*.

Shoes

cross training shoes	**los zapatos de deporte** ***m/pl*** lōs säpä'tōs de depōr'te
heel	**el tacón** el täkōn'
leather	**el cuero** el ko͞o·e'rō
leather sole	**la suela de cuero** lä so͞o·e'lä de ko͞o·e'rō
mountain boots	**las botas de montaña** ***f/pl*** läs bō'täs de mōntä'nyä
pumps	**los zapatos de tacón** ***m/pl*** lōs säpä'tōs de täkōn'
rubber sole	**la suela de goma** lä so͞o·e'lä de gō'mä
sandals	**las sandalias** ***f/pl*** läs sändä'lyäs
shoe polish	**la crema para zapatos** lä kre'mä pä'rä säpä'tōs
shoelaces	**los cordones** ***m/pl*** lōs kōrdō'nes
shoes	**los zapatos** lōs säpä'tōs
size	**el número** el no͞o'merō
slippers	**las zapatillas** ***f/pl*** läs säpätē'lyäs
suede	**el ante** el än'te
tight	**estrecho** estre'tshō

WATCHES AND JEWELRY

My watch is *fast/slow.* **Mi reloj** ***adelanta/atrasa.***
mē relōh' *ädelän'tä/äträ'sä.*

I'm looking for a pretty *souvenir/present.* **Estoy buscando un** ***recuerdo/regalo*** **bonito.** estoi' bo͞oskän'dō o͞on *reko͞o·er'dō/regä'lō* bōnē'to.

? **¿De qué precio?** In what price range?
¿de ke pre'syō?

What's this made of? **¿De qué material es?**
¿de ke mäterē·äl' es?

Watches and Jewelry

alarm clock	**el despertador** el despertädōr'
battery	**la pila** lä pē'lä
bracelet	**la pulsera** lä pōōlse'rä
brooch	**el prendedor ⟨Sp: el broche⟩** el prendedōr' ⟨Sp: el brō'tshe⟩
costume jewelry	**la bisutería** lä bēsōōterē'ä
cuff links	**los gemelos** ***m/pl*** **⟨Mex: las mancuernas** ***f/pl*⟩** lōs heme'lōs ⟨Mex: läs mänkōō·er'näs⟩
earclips	**los aretes** ***m/pl*** lōs äre'tes
earrings	**los pendientes** ***m/pl*** lōs pendyen'tes
gold	**el oro** el ō'rō
gold-plated	**dorado** dōrä'dō
necklace	**el collar** el colyär'
pearl	**la perla** lä per'lä
pendant	**el colgante** el kōlgän'te
ring	**el anillo** el änē'lyō
silver	**la plata** lä plä'tä
silver-plated	**plateado** pläte·ä'dō
watch	**el reloj** el relōh'
watchband	**la pulsera de reloj** lä pōōlse'rä de relōh'

PERSONAL HYGIENE AND HOUSEHOLD

6

Personal Hygiene (word list)

aftershave	**el after shave** el äf'ter shev
baby bottle	**el biberón** el bē'berōn'
baby bottle nipple	**la tetina** lä tetē'nä
baby oil	**el aceite para bebés** el äse'ēte pä'rä bebes'
baby powder	**los polvos para bebés** ***m/pl*** lōs pōl'vōs pä'rä bebes'
body lotion	**la loción corporal** lä lōsyōn' kōrpōräl'
brush	**el cepillo** el sepē'lyō
cleansing cream	**la leche limpiadora** lä le'tshe lēmpyädō'rä
comb	**el peine ⟨Co: la peinilla, Chi: la peineta⟩** el pe'ēne ⟨Co: lä pe·ēnē'lyä, Chi: lä pe·ēne'tä⟩
condoms	**los condones** lōs kōndō'nes
cotton balls	**los algodones** ***m/pl*** lōs älgōdō'nes
cotton swabs	**los bastoncillos** ***m/pl*** lōs bästōnsē'lyōs
dandruff shampoo	**el champú anticaspa** el tshämpōō äntēkäs'pä
deodorant	**el desodorante** el desōdōrän'te
diapers	**los pañales** ***m/pl*** lōs pänyä'les
eye liner	**el trazado de párpado** el träsä'dō de pär'pädō

eye shadow	**la sombra de ojos** lä sōm'brä de ō'h̲ōs
fragrance-free	**sin perfume** sēn perfo͞o'me
hair dryer	**el secador** el sekädōr'
hair pins	**las horquillas** ***f/pl*** läs ōrkē'lyäs
hair mousse	**la espuma para el pelo** lä espo͞o'mä pä'rä el pe'lō
hair spray	**la laca** lä lä'kä
hair styling gel	**el fijador** el fēh̲ädōr'
hand cream	**la crema para las manos** lä kre'mä pä'rä läs mä'nōs
lipstick	**el lápiz de labios ⟨Co, Par: el colorete⟩** el lä'pēs de lä'byōs ⟨Co, Par: el kōlōre'te⟩
makeup	**el maquillaje** el mäkēlyä'h̲e
mascara	**la pestañina ⟨Sp: el rímel⟩** lä pestänyē'nä ⟨Sp: el rē'mel⟩
mirror	**el espejo** el espe'h̲ō
moisturizer	**la crema de hidratación** lä kre'mä de ēdrätäsyōn'
mosquito repellent	**la protección contra los mosquitos** lä prōteksyōn' kōn'trä lōs mōskē'tōs
nail file	**la lima de uñas** lä lē'mä de o͞o'nyäs
nail polish	**el esmalte** el esmäl'te
nail polish remover	**el quitaesmalte** el kētä·esmäl'te
pacifier	**el chupete** el tsho͞ope'te
perfume	**el perfume** el perfo͞o'me
pH balanced	**ph-neutro** pe-ä'tshe-ne'o͞otrō
plaster	**el esparadrapo** el espärädrä'pō
powder	**los polvos** ***m/pl*** lōs pōl'vōs

6

razor *(electric)*	**la máquina de afeitar eléctrica** lä mä'kēnä de äfe·ētär' elek'trēkä
razor *(safety)*	**la rasuradora ⟨Sp: la maquinilla de afeitar⟩** lä räsōōrädō'rä ⟨Sp: lä mäkēnē'lyä de äfe·ētär'⟩
razor blade	**la hoja de afeitar** lä ō'h̲ä de äfe·ētär'
rouge	**el colorete** el kōlōre'te
sanitary napkins	**las toallas sanitarias *f/pl* ⟨Sp: las compresas *f/pl*⟩** läs tō·ä'lyäs sänētär'yäs ⟨Sp: läs kōmpre'säs⟩
shampoo	**el champú** el tshämpōō'
shampoo for *dry/oily* hair	**el champú para cabello *seco/graso*** el tshämpōō' pä'rä käbe'lyō *se'kō/grä'sō*
shaving cream	**la crema de afeitar** lä kre'mä de äfe·ētär'
skin cream	**la crema para la piel** lä kre'mä pä'rä lä pyel'
soap	**el jabón** el h̲äbōn'
sunblock	**el filtro solar** el fēl'trō sōlär'
sun protection factor	**el factor de protección contra el sol** el fäktōr' de prōteksyōn' kōn'trä el sōl
suntan oil	**el aceite solar ⟨Mex: el bronceador⟩** el äse'ēte sōlär' ⟨Mex: el brōnse·ädōr'⟩
tampons	**los tampones *m/pl*** lōs tämpō'nes
tissues	**los pañuelos de papel** lōs pänyōō·e'lōs de päpel'
toilet tissue	**el papel higiénico** el päpel' ēh̲ē·e'nēkō
toothbrush	**el cepillo de dientes** el sepē'lyō de dyen'tes

toothpaste	**la pasta dentífrica** lä päs'tä dentē'frēkä
tweezers	**las pinzas** ***f/pl*** läs pēn'säs
washcloth	**la manopla de baño** lä mänō'plä de bän'yō

Household Items

alarm clock	**el despertador** el despertädōr'
aluminum foil	**el papel de aluminio** el päpel' de äloomē'nyō
battery	**la pila** lä pē'lä
bottle opener	**el destapador ⟨Sp: el abridor⟩** el destäpädōr' ⟨Sp: el äbrēdōr'⟩
can opener	**el abrelatas** el äbrelä'täs
candle	**la vela** lä ve'lä
charcoal	**el carbón para la parrilla** el kärbōn' pä'rä lä pärē'lyä
clothes pins	**las pinzas** ***f/pl*** läs pēn'säs
corkscrew	**el sacacorchos** el säkäkōr'tshōs
cup	**la taza** lä tä'sä
detergent	**el detergente** el deterhen'te
extension cord	**el alargador** el älärgädōr'
flashlight	**la linterna ⟨Mex: el foco de mano⟩** lä lēnter'nä ⟨Mex: el fō'kō de mä'nō⟩
fork	**el tenedor** el tenedōr'
glass *(drinking)*	**el vaso** el vä'sō
grill	**la parrilla** lä pärē'lyä
immersion heater	**el calentador de inmersión** el kälentädōr' de enmersyōn'

6

insect repellent	**el insecticida** el ēnsektēsē'dä
kitchen towel	**el paño de cocina** el pä'nyō de kōsē'nä
knife	**el cuchillo** el ko͞otshē'lyō
light bulb	**el bombillo ⟨Mex: el foco, Sp: la bombilla⟩** el bōmbē'lyō ⟨Mex: el fō'kō, Sp: lä bōmbē'lyä⟩
lighter	**el encendedor ⟨Sp: el mechero⟩** el ensendedōr' ⟨Sp: el metshe'rō⟩
matches	**los fósforos ⟨Mex: los cerillos, Sp: las cerillas⟩** lōs fōs'fōrōs ⟨Mex: lōs serē'-lyōs, Sp: läs serē'lyäs⟩
mosquito net	**el mosquitero** el mōskēte'rō
napkins	**las servilletas** ***f/pl*** läs servēlye'täs
pan	**la sartén** lä särten'
paper cup	**el vaso de papel** el vä'sō de päpel'
paper plate	**el plato de papel** el plä'tō de päpel'
paper towels	**el papel de cocina** el päpel' de kōsē'nä
pin	**el alfiler** el älfēler'
plastic cutlery	**los cubiertos de plástico** ***m/pl*** lōs ko͞obē·er'tōs de pläs'tēkō
plastic wrap	**el plástico de conservación** el pläs'tēkō de kōnserväsyōn'
plate	**el plato** el plä'tō
pocket knife	**la navaja** lä nävä'h̲ä
pot	**la olla** lä o'lyä
rag	**el trapo** el trä'pō
safety pin	**el imperdible ⟨Mex: el seguro⟩** el ēmperdē'ble ⟨Mex: el sego͞o'rō⟩
scissors	**las tijeras** ***f/pl*** läs tēh̲e'räs

sewing needle	**la aguja de coser** lä ägo͞o'h̲ä de cōser'
spoon	**la cuchara** lä ko͞otshä'rä
string	**la cuerda** lä ko͞o·er'dä
thread	**el hilo de coser** el ē'lō de kōser'
toothpicks	**los palillos** ***m/pl*** lōs pälē'lyōs

AT THE OPTICIAN'S

My glasses are broken. **Se me han roto los lentes ⟨Sp: las gafas⟩.** se me än rō'tō lōs len'tes ⟨Sp: läs gä'fäs⟩.

Can you fix them? **¿*Las*/*los* puede arreglar?** ¿*läs*/*lōs* po͞o·e'de äreglär'?

I'm *nearsighted*/*farsighted*. **Soy *miope*/*présbita*.** soi *mē·ō'pe*/*pres'bētä*.

? **¿Cuántas dioptrías tiene usted?** ¿ko͞o·än'täs dē·ōptrē'äs tye'ne o͞oste'? Do you know your prescription?

I have ... dioptres in the right eye and ... in the left. **Tengo en el ojo derecho ... dioptrías y en el izquierdo ... dioptrías.** teng'gō en el ō'h̲ō dere'tshō ... dē·ōptrē'äs ē en el ēskyer'dō ... dē·ōptrē'äs.

I'd like a pair of sunglasses (with graduated lenses). **Quiero unos lentes ⟨Sp: unas gafas⟩ de sol (con los cristales graduados).** kye'rō o͞o'nōs len'tes ⟨Sp: o͞o'näs gä'fäs⟩ de sōl (kōn lōs krēstä'les grädo͞o·ä'dōs).

I've lost my contact lenses.	**He perdido mis lentes de contacto ⟨Sp: mis lentillas⟩.** e perdē'dō mēs len'tes de kōntäk'tō ⟨Sp: mēs lentē'lyäs⟩.
I've broken my contact lenses.	**Los lentes de contacto ⟨Sp: las lentillas⟩ se me han rotos/rotas.** lōs len'tes de kōntäk'tō ⟨Sp: läs lentē'-lyäs⟩ se me än rō'tōs/rō'täs.
I need some *rinsing/ cleaning* solution for *hard/ soft* contact lenses.	**Necesito líquido para *conservar/ limpiar* los lentes de contacto *duros/ blandos.*** nesesē'tō lē'kēdō pä'rä *kōnservär'/lēmpyär'* lōs len'tes de kōntäk'tō *dōō'rōs/ blän'dōs.*

6

AT THE HAIRDRESSER'S

I'd like to make an appointment for…	**Quisiera pedir hora para…** kēsye'rä pedēr' ō'rä pä'rä…
? **¿Qué se va hacer?** ¿ke se vä äser'?	What would you like to have done?
Just a *cut/ trim*, please.	***Cortar/ sólo las puntas*, por favor.** *kōrtär'/sō'lō läs pōōn'täs*, pōr fävōr'.
Wash, cut and blow-dry, please.	**Lavar, cortar y secar, por favor.** lävär', kōrtär' ē sekär', pōr fävōr'.
I'd like…	**Quisiera…** kēsye'rä…
a permanent.	**una permanente.** ōō'nä permänen'te.

some highlights put in.	**mechas.** me'tshäs.
a manicure.	**una manicura** o͞o'nä mänēko͞o'rä
my hair tinted.	**dar reflejos al pelo.** där refle'h̲ōs äl pe'lō.

? **¿Cómo le gustaría?** ¿kō'mō le go͞ostärē'ä? — How would you like it?

Not too short, please.	**Por favor, no muy corto.** pōr fävōr', nō mo͞o'ē kōr'tō.
A little shorter, please.	**Por favor, un poco más corto.** pōr fävōr', o͞on pō'kō mäs kōr'tō.
Please cut a little more…	**Por favor, córteme un poco más…** pōr fävōr', kōr'teme o͞on pō'kō mäs…
on the sides.	**a los lados.** ä lōs lä'dōs.
in the back.	**por detrás.** pōr deträs'.
on the top.	**arriba.** ärē'bä.
in the front.	**por delante.** pōr delän'te.
Part it on the *left/ right,* please.	**La línea ⟨Sp: la raya⟩ a la *izquierda/ derecha.*** lä lē'ne·ä ⟨Sp: lä rä'yä⟩ ä lä *ēskyer' dä / dere' tshä.*
Please cut my beard.	**Por favor, recórteme la barba.** pōr fävōr', rekōr'teme lä bär'bä.
Please give me a shave.	**Por favor, afeitar.** pōr fävōr, äfe·ētär'.

At the Hairdresser's

bangs	**el flequillo** el flekē'lyō
beard	**la barba** lä bär'bä
blond hair	**pelo rubio** pe'lō ro͞o'byō
to blow-dry	**secar** sekär'
brown hair	**pelo castaño** pe'lō kästä'nyō
to cut	**cortar** kōrtär'
dry hair	**el pelo seco** el pe'lō se'kō
dye	**teñir** tenyēr'
hair	**el pelo** el pe'lō
hair spray	**la laca** lä lä'kä
hairdo	**el peinado** el pe·ēnä'dō
hairpiece	**el postizo** el pōstē'sō
manicure	**la manicura** lä mänēko͞o'rä
moustache	**el bigote** el bēgō'te
oily hair	**el pelo graso** el pe'lō grä'sō
part	**la línea** ⟨**Sp: la raya**⟩ lä lē'ne·ä ⟨Sp: lä rä'yä⟩
permanent	**la permanente** lä permänen'te
razor cut	**el corte a navaja** el kōr'te ä nävä'h̲ä
to shave	**afeitar** äfe·ētär'
to tint	**dar reflejos** där refle'h̲ōs
to wash	**lavar** lävär'

PHOTO AND VIDEO

I'd like…	**Quisiera…** kēsye'rä…
a memory card.	**una tarjeta de memoria.** oo'nä tärhe'tä de memō'ryä.
a roll of *color print film/black and white film.*	**un rollo ⟨Sp: un carrete⟩ en *color/blanco y negro.*** o͞on rō'lyō ⟨Sp: o͞on käre'te⟩ en *kōlōr'/bläng'kō ē ne'grō.*
a roll of slide film.	**un rollo de transparencias ⟨Sp: un carrete de diapositivas⟩** o͞on rō'lyō de tränspären'syäs ⟨Sp: o͞on käre'te de dē·äpōsētē'väs⟩.
a *24/36* exposure film.	**un rollo ⟨Sp: un carrete⟩ de *veinticuatro/treinta y seis* fotos.** o͞on ro'lyō ⟨Sp: o͞on käre'te⟩ de *ve·ēntēko͞o·ä'trō/tre'ēntä ē se'ēs* fō'tōs.
Can this video cassette be used on NTSC video recorders?	**¿Se puede utilizar este videocasete en videograbadoras NTSC?** ¿se po͞o·e'de o͞otēlēsär' es'te vēde·ōkäse'te en vēde·ōgräbädō'räs e'ne-te-e'se-se?
I'd like some batteries for this camera.	**Quisiera pilas para este aparato.** kēsye'rä pē'läs pä'rä es'te äpärä'tō.
Could you please put in the roll of film for me?	**¿Me puede poner el rollo ⟨Sp: el carrete⟩?** ¿me po͞o·e'de pōner' el rō'lyō ⟨Sp: el käre'te⟩?

I'd like to get this roll of film developed.	**¿Pueden revelarme este rollo ⟨Sp: carrete⟩?** ¿pōō·e'den revelär'me es'te rō'lyō ⟨Sp: käre'te⟩?
Just the negatives, please.	**Por favor, sólo los negativos.** pōr fävōr', sō'lō lōs negätē'vōs.
Please make a ... by ... print of each negative.	**Por favor, de cada negativo una copia de ... por ...** pōr fävōr', de kä'dä negätē'vō ōō'nä kō'pyä de ... pōr ...
When will the pictures be ready?	**¿Cuándo estarán listas las fotos?** ¿kōō·än'dō estärän' lēs'täs läs fō'tōs?
Can you repair my camera?	**¿Pueden arreglarme la cámara fotográfica?** ¿pōō·e'den äreglär'me lä kä'märä fōtogrä'fēkä?
The film doesn't wind forward.	**No transporta.** nō tränspōr'tä.
The *shutter release/ flash* doesn't work.	**El *disparador/flash* no funciona.** *el dēspärädōr' / el fläsh* nō fōōnsyō'nä.
I need to have passport photos made.	**Quisiera hacerme fotos de pasaporte.** kēsye'rä äser'me fō'tōs de päsäpōr'te.
Do you have any *tapes/CDs* by ...?	**¿Tienen *casetes/CDs* de ...?** ¿tye'nen *käse'tes/sedes'* de ...?
I'd like the most recent cassette by ...	**Quisiera el casete más reciente de ...** kēsye'rä el käse'te mäs resyen'te de ...

6

I like traditional music very much.	**Me interesa mucho la música tradicional.** me ēntere'sä mo͞o'tshō lä mo͞o'sēkä trädēsyōnäl'.
What can you recommend?	**¿Qué puede usted recomendarme?** ¿ke po͞o·e'de o͞oste' rekōmendär'me?

Photo and Video

battery	**la pila** lä pē'lä
black and white film	**el rollo ⟨Sp: el carrete⟩ en blanco y negro** el rō'lyō ⟨Sp: el käre'te⟩ en bläng'kō ē ne'grō
camcorder	**el camcorder** el kämkōrder'
camera	**la máquina fotográfica** lä mä'kēnä fōtōgrä'fēkä
CDs	**los CDs** ***m/pl*** lōs sedes'
color film	**el rollo ⟨Sp: el carrete⟩ de color** el rō'lyō ⟨Sp: el käre'te⟩ de kōlōr'
color filter	**el filtro de color** el fēl'trō de kōlōr'
to develop	**revelar** revelär'
digital camera	**la camara digital** lä kä'merä dehētäl
enlargement	**la ampliación** lä ämplēäsyōn'
exposure meter	**el exposímetro** el ekspōsē'metrō
to film	**filmar** fēlmär'
film camera	**la filmadora ⟨Sp: la cámara⟩** lä fēlmädō'rä ⟨Sp: lä kä'märä⟩
flash	**el flash** el fläsh
lens	**el objectivo** el ōbhetē'vō
music	**la música** lä mo͞o'sēkä
negative	**el negativo** el negätē'vō

photograph	**la fotografía** lä fōtōgräfē'ä
radio	**el/la radio** el/lä rä'dyō
shutter (release)	**el disparador** el dēspärädōr'
slide	**la transparencia ⟨Sp: la diapositiva⟩** lä tränspären'syä ⟨Sp: lä dē·äpōsētē'vä⟩
slide film	**el rollo ⟨Sp: el carrete⟩ de transparencias** el rō'lyō ⟨Sp: el käre'te⟩ de tränspären'syäs
telephoto lens	**el teleobjetivo** el tele·ōbhetē'vō
ultraviolet filter	**el filtro-UV** el fēl'trō-ōō-ve'
video camera	**la videocámara** lä vēde·ōkä'märä
video cassette	**el videocasete** el vēde·ōkäse'te
wide angle lens	**el objetivo gran angular** el ōbhetē'vō grän äng·gōōlär'
zoom lens	**el zoom** el sōōm

READING AND WRITING

I'd like … **Quisiera …** kēsye'rä …

a U.S. newspaper. **un periódico de los Estados Unidos.** ōōn pere·ō'dēkō de lōs estä'dōs ōōnē'dōs.

a U.S. magazine. **una revista de los Estados Unidos.** ōō'nä revēs'tä de lōs estä'dōs ōōnē'dōs.

a map of the surrounding area. **un mapa de los alrededores.** ōōn mä'pä de lōs älrededō'res.

Do you have books in English?	**¿Tienen libros en inglés?** ¿tye'nen lē'brōs en ēng·gles'?

Reading and Writing

adhesive tape	**la cinta adhesiva** lä sēn'tä ädesē'vä
airmail paper	**el papel para cartas por avión** el päpel' pä'rä kär'täs pōr ävyōn'
ballpoint pen	**la pluma ⟨Sp: el bolígrafo⟩** lä plo͞o'mä ⟨Sp: el bōlē'gräfō⟩
bike map	**el mapa de rutas en bicicleta** el mä'pä de ro͞o'täs en bēsēklē'tä
board game	**el juego de sociedad** el h͟o͞o·e'gō de sōsyedäd'
book	**el libro** el lē'brō
city map	**el plano de la ciudad** el plä'nō de lä syo͞odäd'
colored pencil	**el lápiz de color** el lä'pēs de kōlōr'
coloring book	**el libro para colorear** el lē'brō pä'rä kōlōrē·är'
cookbook	**el libro de cocina** el lē'brō de kōsē'nä
dictionary	**el diccionario** el dēksyōnär'yō
envelope	**el sobre** el sō'bre
eraser	**la goma** lä gō'mä
glue	**el pegamento** el pegämen'tō
hiking trail map	**el mapa de excursiones** el mä'pä de eksko͞orsyō'nes
magazine	**la revista** lä revēs'tä
newspaper	**el periódico** el perē·ō'dēkō
notepad	**el bloc de notas** el blōk de nō'täs

paper	**el papel** el päpel'
pencil	**el lápiz** el lä'pēs
picture book	**el libro con ilustraciones** el lē'brō kōn ēlōōsträsyō'nes
playing cards	**las cartas para jugar** ***f/pl*** läs kär'täs pä'rä h̲ōōgär'
postcard	**la tarjeta postal** lä tärh̲e'tä pōstäl'
road map	**el mapa de carreteras** el mä'pä de kärete'räs
stamp	**la estampilla ⟨Mex: el timbre, Sp: el sello⟩** lä estämpē'lyä ⟨Mex: el tēm'bre, Sp: el se'lyō⟩
travel guide	**la guía de viaje** lä gē'ä de vyä'h̲e
writing paper	**el papel para cartas** el päpel' pä'rä kär'täs

6

AT THE TOBACCONIST'S

A pack of cigarettes *with/without* filter, please.	**Un paquete ⟨Mex: una cajetilla⟩ de cigarrillos ⟨Mex: cigarros⟩ *con/sin* filtro, por favor.** ōōn päke'te ⟨Mex: ōō'nä käh̲etē'lyä⟩ de sēgärē'lyōs ⟨Mex: sēgä'rōs⟩ *kōn/sēn* fel'tro, pōr fävōr'.
A pack/A carton of…, please.	**Por favor, *un paquete* ⟨Mex: *una cajetilla*⟩ / *un cartón* de…** pōr fävōr', *ōōn päke'te* ⟨Mex: *ōō'nä käh̲etē'lyä*⟩ / *ōōn kärtōn'* de…

Five cigars, please.	**Cinco cigarros puros ⟨Sp: puros⟩, por favor.** sēng'kō segä'rōs po͞o'rōs ⟨Sp: po͞o'rōs⟩, pōr fävōr'.
A can of pipe tobacco, please.	**Por favor, una caja de tabaco de pipa.** pōr fävōr', o͞o'nä kä'hä de täbä'kō de pē'pä.
Could I have *some matches/a lighter*, please?	**Por favor, *unos fósforos* ⟨Mex: *cerrillos*, Sp: *cerillas*⟩ / *un encendedor* ⟨Sp: *un mechero*⟩.** pōr fävōr', *o͞o'nōs fōs'fōrōs* ⟨Mex: *serē'lyōs*, Sp: *serē'lyäs*⟩ / *o͞on ensendedōr'* ⟨Sp: *o͞on metshe'rō*⟩.

Entertainment and Sports

SWIMMING AND WATER SPORTS

At the Beach

Is there a *sand/rock* beach around here?	**¿Hay por aquí cerca una playa de *arena/piedras*?** ¿ī pōr äkē' ser'kä o͞o'nä plä'yä de *äre'nä/pye'dräs*?
How do I get to the beach?	**¿Por dónde se va a la playa?** ¿pōr dōn'de se vä ä lä plä'yä?
Can I rent beach *umbrellas/awnings*?	**¿Se puede rentar ⟨Sp: alquilar⟩ allí *sombrillas/toldos*?** ¿se po͞o·e'de rentär' ⟨Sp: älkēlär'⟩ älyē' *sōmbrē'lyäs/tōl'dōs*?
Is there any shade?	**¿Hay algún sitio con sombra?** ¿ī älgo͞on' sē'tyō kōn sōm'brä?
Is swimming permitted here?	**¿Se puede bañarse aquí?** ¿se po͞o·e'de bänyär'se äkē'?

! **¡Prohibido bañarse!** ¡prōēbē'dō bänyär'se! — No swimming!

How *deep/warm* is the water?	**¿Qué *profundidad/temperatura* tiene el agua?** ke *prōfo͞ondēdäd'/temperäto͞o'rä* tye'ne el ä'go͞o·ä?
Are there currents here?	**¿Hay aquí corrientes?** ¿ī äkē' kōryen'tes?
Is it dangerous for children?	**¿Es peligroso para los niños?** ¿es pelēgrō'so pä'rä lōs nē'nyōs?

Are there jellyfish around here?	**¿Hay medusas por aquí?** ¿ī medōō'säs pōr äkē'?
Where can I rent…?	**¿Dónde se puede rentar ⟨Sp: alquilar⟩ …?** ¿dōn'de se pōō·e'de rentär' ⟨Sp: älkēlär'⟩ …?
I would like to rent a *beach chair / beach umbrella.*	**Quisiera rentar ⟨Sp: alquilar⟩ una *tumbona / sombrilla.*** kēsye'rä rentär' ⟨Sp: älkēlär'⟩ ōō'nä *tōōmbō'nä / sōmbrē'lyä.*
I'd like to go waterskiing.	**Quiero hacer esquí acuático.** kye'rō äser' eskē' äkōō·ä'tēkō.
I'd like to take *diving / windsurfing* lessons.	**Quiero hacer un curso de *submarinismo / windsurfing.*** kye'rō äser' ōōn kōōr'sō de *sōōbmärēnēz'mō / ōō·ēn'sōōrfēng.*

INFO The long coastlines of Mexico and Central America, on both the Caribbean and Pacific sides, are world famous for all water and beach activities including swimming, windsurfing, waterskiing, diving, snorkling, boating and deep sea fishing. Don't forget to protect yourself from the sun.

Can I go on a fishing boat?	**¿Se puede ir en un barco pesquero?** ¿se pōō·e'de ēr en ōōn bär'kō peske'rō?
How much is it *per hour / per day*?	**¿Cuánto cuesta *por hora / por día*?** ¿kōō·än'tō kōō·es'tä *pōr ō'rä / pōr dē'ä*?

Would you mind keeping an eye on my things for a moment, please?	**Por favor, ¿podría cuidar ⟨Sp: vigilar⟩ mis cosas un momento?** pōr fävōr', ¿pōdrē'ä ko͞o·ēdär' ⟨Sp: vēh̲ēlär'⟩ mēs kō'säs o͞on mōmen'tō?

At the Swimming Pool

How much is the entrance ticket?	**¿Cuánto cuesta el boleto ⟨Sp: la entrada⟩?** ¿ko͞o·än'tō ko͞o·es'tä el bōle'tō ⟨Sp: lä enträ'dä⟩?
What coins do I need for the *lockers/ hairdryers*?	**¿Qué monedas se necesitan para *la consigna/el secador*?** ¿ke mōne'däs se nesesē'tän pä'rä *lä kōnsēg'nä/el sekädōr'*?
Is there a sauna?	**¿Hay una sauna?** ¿ī co͞o'nä sou'nä?
Where's the *lifeguard/ first-aid station*?	**¿Dónde está *el vigilante/el puesto de socorros*?** ¿dōn'de estä' *el vēh̲ēlän'te/ el po͞o·es'tō de sōkō'rōs*?

Swimming and Water Sports

air mattress	**el colchón de aire (hinchable) ⟨Sp: la colchoneta⟩** el kōltshōn' de ī're (ēntshä'ble) ⟨Sp: lä kōltshōne'tä⟩
bathing suit	**el traje de baño** el trä'h̲e de bä'nyō
bay	**la bahía** lä bä·ē'ä
beach	**la playa** lä plä'yä
beach chair	**la tumbona** lä to͞ombō'nä

beach shoes	**las zapatillas de baño** ***f/pl*** läs säpätē'lyäs de bä'nyō
beach umbrella	**la sombrilla** lä sōmbrē'lyä
bikini	**el bikini** el bēkē'nē
boat	**el barco** el bär'kō
boat rental	**el alquiler de barcos** el älkēler' de bär'kōs
changing rooms	**los vestuarios** ***m/pl*** lōs vesto͞o·är'yōs
to dive	**bucear** bo͞ose·är'
diving board	**el trampolín** el trämpōlēn'
diving equipment	**el equipo de buceo** el ekē'pō de bo͞ose'ō
diving mask	**el visor ⟨Sp: las gafas** ***f/pl*****⟩ de buceo** el vēsōr' ⟨Sp: läs gä'fäs⟩ de bo͞ose'ō
diving suit	**la escafandra** lä eskäfän'drä
fins	**las aletas** ***f/pl*** läs äle'täs
to fish	**pescar** peskär'
fishing boat	**el barco pesquero** el bär'kō peske'rō
fishing rod	**la caña de pescar** lä kä'nyä de peskär'
to go swimming *(as a sport)*	**nadar** nädär'
to go swimming *(for pleasure)*	**bañarse** bänyär'se
hot springs	**los aguas termales** ***f/pl*** lōs ä'go͞o·äs termä'les
inflatable dinghy	**el bote neumático** el bō'te ne·oomä'tēkō
jellyfish	**la medusa** lä medo͞o'sä
lifebelt	**el salvavidas** el sälvävē'däs

motorboat	**la lancha con motor ⟨Mex: el motonauta⟩** lä län'tshä kōn mōtōr' ⟨Mex: el mōtonou'tä⟩
non-swimmer	**el no-nadador** el nō nädädōr'
nude beach	**la playa nudista** lä plä'yä nōōdēs'tä
pedal boat	**el patín ⟨Sp: el velomar⟩** el pätēn' ⟨Sp: el velōmär'⟩
rocks	**las rocas *f/pl*** läs rō'käs
rowboat	**el bote de remos** el bō'te de re'mōs
to sail	**hacer vela** äser' ve'lä
sailboat	**el barco de vela** el bär'kō de ve'lä
sand	**la arena** lä äre'nä
sandy beach	**la playa de arena** lä plä'yä de äre'nä
sea urchin	**el erizo de mar** el erē'sō de mär
shade	**la sombra** lä sōm'brä
shells	**las conchas *f/pl*** läs kōn'tshäs
shower	**la regadera ⟨Sp: la ducha⟩** lä regäde'rä ⟨Sp: lä dōō'tshä⟩
snorkel	**el esnórquel** el esnōr'kel
storm	**la tempestad** lä tempestäd'
storm warning	**el aviso de tempestad** el ävē'sō de tempestäd'
sun	**el sol** el sōl
sunblock	**el filtro solar** el fēl'trō sōlär'
sunglasses	**los lentes *m/pl* ⟨Sp: las gafas *f/pl*⟩ de sol** lōs len'tes ⟨Sp: läs gä'fäs⟩ de sōl
surfboard	**la tabla de surf** lä tä'blä de sōōrf

swim goggles	**las gafas protectoras (de inmersión)** ***f/pl*** läs gä'fäs prōtek'tōräs (de ēnmersyōn')
swim trunks	**el pantalón de baño ⟨Sp: el bañador⟩** el päntälōn' de bä'nyō ⟨Sp: el bänyädōr'⟩
swimming pool	**la alberca ⟨Sp: la piscina⟩** lä älber'kä ⟨Sp: lä pēsē'nä⟩
towel	**la toalla** lä tō·ä'lyä
water	**el agua** el ä'go͞o·ä
water polo	**el polo acuático** el pō'lō äko͞o·ä'tēkō
water ski	**el esquí acuático** el eskē' äko͞o·ä'tēkō
water wings	**los flotadores *m/pl*** lōs flōtädō'res
wave	**la ola** lä ō'lä
wetsuit	**la escafandra** lä eskäfän'drä

MOUNTAINEERING

I'd like to *go to/climb* …	**Quisiera *ir a/subir al*…** kēsy'erä *ēr ä/so͞obēr' äl*…
Can you recommend *an easy/a moderately difficult* (hiking) trail?	**¿Puede usted recomendarme una ruta *fácil/más difícil*?** ¿po͞o·e'de o͞oste' rekōmendär'me o͞o'nä ro͞o'tä *fä'sēl/mäs dēfē'sēl*?
Is the path well *marked/secured*?	**¿Está bien *señalado/asegurado* el camino?** ¿estä byen' *senyälä'dō/äsego͞orä'dō* el kämē'nō?

Are there trips with guides?	**¿Hay excursiones con guías?** ¿ī eskōōrsy·ō'nes kōn gē'äs?
At what time does the *next/last* cable car leave (*going up/going down*)?	**¿A qué hora sale el *próximo/último* funicular (*para arriba/para abajo*)?** ¿ä ke ō'rä sä'le el *prō'ksēmō/ōōl'tēmō* fōōnēkōōlär' (*pä'rä ärē'bä/pä'rä äbä'hō*)?
Is this the right way to …?	**¿Es éste el camino correcto para …?** ¿es es'te el kämē'nō kōrek'tō pä'rä …?
How much farther is it to …?	**¿Cuánto queda para llegar a …?** ¿kōō·än'tō ke'dä pä'rä lyegär' ä …?

Mountaineering

cable car	**el teleférico** el telefe'rēkō
to climb	**subir a** sōōbēr' ä
hiking boots	**las botas de montaña *f/pl*** läs bō'täs de mōntä'nyä
compass	**la brújula** lä brōō'hōōlä
funicular railway	**el funicular** el fōōnēkōōlär'
to hike	**caminar** kämēnär'
hiking map	**el mapa de rutas de montaña** el mä'pä de rōō'täs de mōntä'nyä
mountain	**la montaña** lä mōntä'nyä
mountain cabin	**el albergue alpino** el älber'ge älpē'nō
mountain guidebook	**el guía de montaña** el gē'ä de mōntä'nyä
mountain range	**la sierra** lä sye'rä
ravine	**el barranco** el bäräng'kō

rope	**la soga** lä sō'gä
ski lift	**el telesilla** el telesē'lyä
trail	**el camino** el kämē'nō

MORE SPORTS AND GAMES

Do you have any *playing cards/board games*?	**¿Tienen *naipes/juegos de sociedad*?** ¿tye'nen *nī'pes/hōō·e'gōs de sōsyedäd'*?
Do you play chess?	**¿Juega usted al ajedrez?** ¿hōō·e'gä ōōste' äl ähedres'?
I'd like to take a course in…	**Quisiera hacer un curso de…** kēsye'rä äser' ōōn kōōr'sō de…
Do you mind if I join in?	**¿Puedo jugar?** ¿pōō·e'dō hōōgär'?

INFO The most popular sport in Latin America is soccer, **fútbol,** which draws enormous, highly excitable crowds. American football is virtually unknown.

We'd like to rent a *tennis court/squash court* for *an hour/half an hour.*	**Nos gustaría utilizar una pista de *tenis/squash* durante *una/media* hora.** nōs gōōstärē'ä ōōtēlēsär' ōō'nä pēs'tä de *te'nēs/skōō·ōsh* dōōrän'te *ōō'nä/me'dyä* ō'rä.
I'd like to rent…	**Quisiera rentar ⟨Sp: alquilar⟩…** kēsye'rä rentär' ⟨Sp: älkēlär'⟩…

athletic	**deportivo** depōrtē'vō
badminton	**el bádminton** el bäd'mēntōn
badminton racket	**la raqueta de bádminton** lä räke'tä de bäd'mēntōn
bait	**el cebo** el se'bō
ball	**la pelota** lä pelō'tä
basketball	**el baloncesto** el bälōnse'stō
beginner	**el/la principiante** el/lä prēnsēpyän'te
bicycle	**la bicicleta** lä bēsēkle'tä
bicycle tour	**la vuelta en bicicleta** lä vo͞o·el'tä en bēsēkle'tä
bowling	**los bolos** ***m/pl*** lōs bō'lōs
bowling alley	**la bolera** lä bōle'rä
canoe	**la canoa** lä känō'ä
changing rooms	**los vestuarios** ***m/pl*** lōs vesto͞o·är'yōs
chess	**el ajedrez** el äh̲edres'
coach	**el entrenador** el entrenädōr'
coaching session	**la hora de entrenamiento** lä ō'rä de entrenämyen'tō
course	**el curso** el ko͞or'sō
defeat	**la derrota** lä derō'tä
double	**el doble** el dō'ble
fencing	**la esgrima** lä ezgrē'mä
final score	**el resultado** el reso͞oltä'dō
finishing line	**la meta** lä me'tä
to fish	**pescar (con caña)** peskär' (kōn kä'nyä)
fishing license	**la licencia de pesca** lä lēsen'syä de pes'kä

fishing rod	**la caña de pescar**	lä kä'nyä de peskär'
game	**el juego**	el h̲o͞o·e'gō
to go by bike	**ir en bicicleta**	ēr en bēsēkle'tä
goal	**el gol**	el gōl
goalkeeper	**el portero**	el pōrte'rō
golf	**el golf**	el gōlf
golf club	**el palo de golf**	el pä'lō de gōlf
golf course	**el campo de golf**	el käm'pō de gōlf
gym	**el gimnasio**	el h̲ēmnä'syō
gymnastics	**la gimnasia**	lä h̲ēmnä'syä
half-time	**el medio tiempo**	el me'dyō tyem'pō
handball	**el balonmano**	el bälōnmä'nō
hang-gliding	**el vuelo en ala-delta**	el vo͞o·e'lō en ä'lä-del'tä
horse	**el caballo**	el käbä'lyō
to jog	**hacer jogging**	äser' yōgēn'
kayak	**el kayak**	el käyäk'
to lose	**perder**	perder'
match	**el juego**	el h̲o͞o·e'gō
minigolf course	**el campo de minigolf**	el käm'pō de mēnēgōlf'
parasailing	**el parapente**	el päräpen'te
to play	**jugar**	h̲o͞ogär'
to ride a horse	**cabalgar**	käbälgär'
single	**el individual**	el ēndēvēdo͞o·äl'
skydiving	**el paracaidismo**	el pärākīdēz'mō
soccer	**el fútbol**	el fo͞ot'bōl

soccer field	**el campo de fútbol** el käm'pō de fo͞ot'bōl
sports	**el deporte** el depōr'te
sports ground	**el polideportivo** el pōlēdepōrtē'vō
starting line	**la salida** lä sälē'dä
table tennis	**el pimpon** el pēmpōn'
team	**el equipo** el ekē'pō
tennis	**el tenis** el te'nēs
tennis court	**la pista de tenis** lä pēs'tä de te'nēs
tennis racket	**la raqueta de tenis** lä räke'tä de te'nēs
to tie the score	**empatar** empätär'
trainer	**el entrenador** el entrenädōr'
victory	**la victoria** lä vēktōr'yä
volleyball	**el voleibol ⟨Sp: el balonvolea⟩** el vōlēbōl' ⟨Sp: el bälōnvōle'ä⟩
to win	**ganar** gänär'

CULTURE AND FESTIVALS

At the Box Office

agotadas las localidades ägōtä'däs läs lōkälēdä'des	sold out
el anfiteatro el änfēte·ä'trō	dress circle
el asiento el äsyen'tō	seat
el boleto el bōle'tō	ticket
la chilla ⟨Sp: el paraíso⟩ lä tshē'lyä ⟨Sp: el päräē'sō⟩	balcony
el descanso el deskän'sō	intermission

la entrada lä enträ'dä	ticket
la fila lä fē'lä	row
la galería lä gälerē'ä	gallery
el guardarropa el gōō·ärdärō'pä	checkroom
el palco el päl'kō	box seat
la platea lä pläte'ä	orchestra seat
la salida de emergencia lä sälē'dä de emerhen'syä	emergency exit
la taquilla lä täkē'lyä	box office
el teatro el te·ä'trō	theater

Do you have a program of cultural activities? **¿Tiene un programa de actividades culturales?** ¿tye'ne ōōn prōgrä'mä de äktēvēdä'des kōōltōōrä'les?

What's on today? **¿Qué ponen hoy?** ¿ke po'nen oi?

Where can I buy tickets? **¿Dónde se puede comprar boletos ⟨Sp: entradas⟩?** ¿dōn'de se pōō·e'de kōmprär' bōle'tōs ⟨Sp: enträ'däs⟩?

INFO Mexico and all of Latin America have a long tradition of folk festivals and **fiestas**. A folk festival can even plunge a town or a village into a state of emergency! For example, one of the most popular Mexican **fiestas** is the Day of the Dead, **el día de los muertos**, (November 2) which takes place in cemeteries and graveyards. People decorate the graves of their relatives with sugar skulls, coffins, tombs and skeletons.

7

When does the *performance/concert* start?	**¿A qué hora empieza *la función/ el concierto*?** ¿ä ke ō'rä empye'sä *lä fo͞onsyōn' / el kōnsyer'tō*?
When do the doors open?	**¿A partir de qué hora se puede entrar?** ¿ä pärtēr' de ke ō'rä se po͞o·e'de enträr'?
Are the seats numbered?	**¿Están numerados los asientos?** ¿estän' no͞omerä'dōs lōs äsyen'tōs?
Can I reserve tickets?	**¿Es posible reservar las entradas?** ¿ es pōsē'ble reservär' läs enträ'däs?

INFO Each area of Mexico has its own dances and dance costumes. Women wear colorful wide skirts and flowers in their hair. Men usually wear a variation of the **charro** (Mexican cowboy) costume. One of the most well-known dances is the Mexican Hat Dance, **el jarabe tapatío**. Here a couple dances around the typical wide-brimmed Mexican **sombrero**. In **La Bamba**, a very famous Mexican wedding dance, the couple makes a bow from a wide white ribbon on the floor using only their feet.

Do you still have tickets for *today/ tomorrow*?	**¿Le quedan boletos ⟨Sp: entradas⟩ para *hoy/mañana*?** ¿le ke'dän bōle'tōs ⟨Sp: enträ'däs⟩ pä'rä *oi/mänyä'nä*?
I'd like two tickets for…	**Por favor, dos boletos ⟨Sp: entradas⟩ para …** pōr fävōr', dōs bōle'tōs ⟨Sp: enträ'däs⟩ pä'rä…

this evening's performance.	**la función de esta tarde.** lä fōōnsyōn' de es'tä tär'de.
tomorrow's performance.	**la función de mañana.** lä fōōnsyōn' de mänyä'nä.
the afternoon performance.	**la función de la tarde.** lä fōōnsyōn' de lä tär'de.
the day after tomorrow.	**pasado mañana.** päsä'dō mänyä'nä.

7

How much is a ticket? **¿Cuánto cuesta un boleto ⟨Sp: una entrada⟩?** ¿kōō·än'tō kōō·es'tä ōōn bōle'tō ⟨Sp: ōō'nä enträ'dä⟩?

Is there a discount for … **¿Hacen descuento a …** ¿ä'sen deskōō·en'tō ä …

children?	**los niños?** lōs nē'nyōs?
senior citizens?	**pensionistas?** pensyōnēs'täs?
students?	**estudiantes?** estōōdyän'tes?

INFO The bullfight, **la corrida de toros**, is little understood by most Americans, yet it is an important part of Hispanic culture. It is not considered to be a sport or a fight but more of a spectacle or ritual. Bullfights are most popular in Mexico, Colombia and Venezuela. Tickets are sold for **sol** (the sunny side of the bullring) or **sombra** (the shady side). The main season is in the winter. Bullfights are usually held on Sunday afternoon at 4 o'clock.

What time does the performance end? **¿A qué hora termina la función?** ¿ä ke ō'rä termē'nä lä fōōnsyōn'?

I'd like to rent some theater glasses.	**Quisiera rentar ⟨Sp: alquilar⟩ unos gemelos.** kēsye'rä rentär' ⟨Sp: älkēlär'⟩ o͞o'nōs heme'lōs.

Culture and Festivals

act	**el acto** el äk'tō
actor	**el actor** el äktōr'
actress	**la actriz** lä äktrēs'
advance booking	**la venta anticipada** lä ven'tä äntēsēpä'dä
ballet	**el ballet** el bälet'
box office	**la taquilla** lä täkē'lyä
bullfight	**la corrida de toros** lä kōrē'dä de tō'rōs
choir	**el coro** el kō'ro
circus	**el circo** el sēr'kō
cloakroom	**el guardarropas** el go͞o·ärdärō'päs
concert	**el concierto** el kōnsyer'tō
concert hall	**la sala de concierto** lä sä'lä de kōnsyer'tō
dancer *(female)*	**la bailarina** lä bīlärē'nä
dancer *(male)*	**el bailarín** el bīlärēn'
discount	**el descuento** el desko͞o·en'tō
dubbed	**doblado** dōblä'dō
end	**el fin** el fēn
folk music recital	**el recital de música folklórica** el resētäl' de mo͞o'sēkä fōlklō'rēkä
intermission	**el descanso** el deskän'sō
leading role	**el papel principal** el päpel' prēnsēpäl'
movie	**la película** lä pelē'ko͞olä

movie theater	**el cine** el sē'ne
music	**la música** lä mo͞o'sēkä
musical	**el musical** el mo͞osēkäl'
open-air theater	**el teatro al aire libre** el te·ä'trō äl ī're lē'bre
opening night	**el estreno** el estre'nō
opera	**la ópera** lä ō'perä
operetta	**la opereta** lä ōpere'tä
orchestra	**la orquesta** lä ōrkes'tä
performance	**la función** lä fo͞onsyōn'
play	**la obra de teatro** lä ō'brä de te·ä'trō
program	**el programa** el prōgrä'mä
seat	**el asiento** el äsyen'tō
singer	**el cantante** el käntän'te
song recital	**el recital de canciones** el resētäl' de känsyō'nes
start	**el comienzo** el kōmyen'sō
subtitle	**el subtítulo** el so͞obtē'to͞olō
subtitled	**con subtítulos** kōn so͞obtē'to͞olōs
theater	**el teatro** el te·ä'trō
ticket	**la entrada** lä enträ'dä
variety show	**la varieté** lä väre·ete'

➡ *Sporting events see also: word list Sports, Games (p. 184)*

GOING OUT IN THE EVENING

Is there a nice bar around here?	**¿Hay por aquí un bar bueno?** ¿ī pōr äkē' o͞on bär bo͞o·e'nō?

7

Where can you go dancing around here?	**¿Adónde se puede ir a bailar?** ¿ädōn'de se pōō·e'de ēr ä bīlär'?
Is this seat free?	**¿Está libre?** ¿estä' lē'bre?
Do you serve meals?	**¿Se puede comer algo aquí?** ¿se pōō·e'de kōmer' äl'gō äkē'?

➡ *Waiter (p. 111)*

Do you have a beverage menu?	**¿Tiene una lista de bebidas?** ¿tye'ne ōō'nä lē'stä de bebē'däs?
I'd like a *beer/glass of wine*, please.	**Me gustaría *una cerveza/una copa de vino*, por favor.** me gōōstärē'ä *ōō'nä serve'sä/ōō'nä kō'pä de vē'nō*, pōr fävōr'.
I'd like another, please.	**Lo mismo otra vez, por favor.** lō mēz'mō ō'trä ves, pōr fävōr'.
What would you like to drink?	**¿Qué *quiere/quieres* tomar ⟨Sp: beber⟩?** ¿ke *kye're/kye'res* tomär' ⟨Sp: beber'⟩?
Can I buy you …?	**Déjeme que le invite a …?** de'heme ke le ēnvē'te ä …?
Would you like to dance?	**¿*Quiere/Quieres* bailar?** ¿*kye're/kye'res* bīlär'?

Post Office, Bank, Internet

POST, TELEGRAMS AND TELEPHONE

Letters and Parcels

Where is the nearest *mailbox/post office*?	**¿Dónde está *el buzón más cercano/la oficina de correos más cercana*?** ¿dōn'de estä' *el bo͞osōn' mäs serkä'nō/ lä ōfēsē'nä de kōre'ōs mäs serkä'nä*?
I'd like to mail this letter…, please.	**Por favor, quisiera enviar esta carta …** pōr fävōr', kēsye'ra envē·är' es'tä kär'tä…
by registered mail	**registrada ⟨Sp: certificada⟩.** reh̲ēsträ'dä ⟨Sp: sertēfēkä'dä⟩.
by airmail	**por avión.** pōr ävyōn'.
by special delivery	**por correo urgente.** pōr kōre'ō o͞orh̲en'te.
How much is the postage for a *letter/ postcard* to the U.S.?	**¿Cuánto cuesta una *carta/tarjeta postal* para los Estados Unidos?** ¿ko͞o·än'tō ko͞o·es'tä o͞o'nä *kär'tä/ tärh̲e'tä pōstäl'* ä lōs estä'dōs o͞onē'dōs?

INFO When sending letters or postcards to the US from Latin America or Spain be sure to specify **por avión** (airmail), otherwise they might be sent by regular mail (**correo ordinario**). In any case, mail is relatively slow.

Five ... stamps, please. **Cinco estampillas ⟨Mex: timbres, Sp: sellos⟩ de ..., por favor.** sēng'kō estämpē'lyäs ⟨Mex: tēm'bres, Sp: se'lyōs⟩ de ..., pōr fävōr'.

I'd like to mail this package. **Quisiera enviar este paquete por correo.** kēsye'rä envēär' es'te päke'te pōr kōre'ō.

Where is the general delivery counter? **¿Dónde está la ventanilla para envíos a la lista de correos?** ¿dōn'de estä' lä ventänē'lyä pä'rä envē'ōs ä lä lēs'tä de kōre'ōs?

Is there any mail for me? **¿Hay correo para mí?** ¿ī kōre'ō pä'är mē?

The Line Home

Can I send a telegram from here? **¿Puedo mandar un telegrama desde aquí?** ¿pōō·e'dō mändär' ōōn telegrä'mä dez'de äkē'?

Can you give me a telegram form? **¿Podría darme un formulario para telegramas?** ¿pōdrē'ä där'me ōōn fōrmōōlär'yō pä'rä telegrä'mäs?

Can I send a fax from here? **¿Se puede enviar un telefax desde aquí?** ¿se pōō·e'de envē·är' ōōn telefäks' des'de äkē'?

8

INFO At the telephone office (**central de teléfonos**; in Mexico **oficina de teléfonos**) you can phone or send a fax. You can pay after your call at the desk or by using coins or a phone card. You can buy phone cards there, too.

Where can I make a phone call?
¿Dónde puedo llamar por teléfono? ¿dōn'de po͞o·e'dō lyämär' pōr tele'fōnō?

Please show me where I can find a telephone booth.
¿Podría indicarme dónde hay una cabina telefónica? pōdrē'ä ēndēkär'me dōn'de ī o͞o'nä käbē'nä tele-fō'nēkä?

! **Vaya a la cabina …** väʼyä ä lä käbē'nä … — Go to booth …

I'd like to pay for my call.
Quisiera pagar mi llamada. kēsye'rä pägär' mē lyämä'dä.

Where can I buy a telephone card?
¿Dónde puedo comprar una tarjeta telefónica? ¿dōn'de po͞o·e'dō kōmprär' o͞o'nä tärhe'tä telefō'nēkä?

Excuse me, could you give me some change to make a phone call?
Perdón, ¿podría darme unas monedas para llamar por teléfono? perdōn', ¿pōdrē'ä där'me o͞o'näs mōne'däs pä'rä lyämär' pōr tele'fōnō?

Could you give me some change for this bill?
¿Podría cambiarme este billete? ¿pōdrē'ä kämbyär'me es'te bēlye'te?

INFO To dial the US direct from Mexico use: 95 + the area code + tel. number.
To dial the US direct from Spain use: 071 + the area code + tel. number.

What's the area code for…?	**¿Cuál es el prefijo de …?** ¿kōō·äl' es el prefē'h̲ō de…?

! **La línea está *ocupada*/ *interrumpida*.** lä lē'ne·ä estä' *ōkōōpä'dä*/ *ēnterrōōmpē'dä*. — The line is *busy*/*out of order*.

! **No contesta nadie.** nō kōntes'tä nä'dye. — There's no answer at that number.

! **Inténtelo otra vez.** ēnten'telō ō'trä ves. — Try again.

8

Post, Telegram, Telephone

address	**la dirección** lä dēreksyōn'
addressee	**el destinatario** el destēnätär'yō
area code	**el prefijo** el prefē'h̲ō
busy	**ocupado** ōkōōpä'dō
by airmail	**por avión** pōr ävyōn'
charge-card phone	**el teléfono de tarjeta** el tele'fōnō de tärh̲e'tä
collect call	**la conferencia a cobro revertido** lä kōnferen'syä ä kō'brō revertē'dō
counter	**la ventanilla** lä ventänē'lyä
cut off *(connection)*	**interrumpido** ēnterrōōmpē'dō

declaration of value	**la declaración de valor** lä dekläräsyōn' de välōr'
to dial	**marcar** märkär'
discount rate	**la tarifa rebajada** lä tärē'fä rebäh̲ä'dä
envelope	**el sobre** el sō'bre
fax	**el telefax** el telefäks'
letter	**la carta** lä kär'tä
local call	**la llamada urbana** lä lyämä'dä o͞orbä'nä
long-distance call	**la llamada ⟨Sp: la conferencia⟩ a larga distancia** lä lyämä'dä ⟨Sp: lä kōnferen'syä⟩ ä lär'gä dēstän'syä
mailbox	**el buzón** el bo͞osōn'
to make a phone call	**llamar por teléfono** lyämär' pōr tele'fōnō
parcel	**el paquete** el päke'te
pay phone	**el teléfono de monedas** el tele'fōnō de mōne'däs
phone	**el teléfono** el tele'fōnō
phone booth	**la cabina telefónica** lä käbē'nä telefō'nēkä
phone call	**la llamada telefónica** lä lyämä'dä telefō'nēkä
post office	**la oficina de correos** lä ōfēsē'nä de kōre'ōs
postcard	**la tarjeta postal** lä tärh̲e'tä pōstäl'
printed matter	**los impresos** ***m/pl*** lōs ēmpre'sōs
to put through to	**poner con** pōner' kōn

to send	**enviar** envyär'
sender	**el remitente** el remēten'te
stamp	**la estampilla** ⟨**Mex: el timbre, Sp: el sello**⟩ lä estämpē'lyä ⟨Mex: el tēm'bre, Sp: el se'lyō⟩
to stamp	**franquear** fränke·är'
telegram	**el telegrama** el telegrä'mä
telephone card	**la tarjeta telefónica** lä tärhe'tä telefō'nēkä
telephone directory	**la guía telefónica** lä gē'ä telefō'nēkä
telephone office	**la oficina telefónica** lä ōfēsē'nä telefō'nēkä

8

MONEY MATTERS

Excuse me, is there a bank around here? — **Perdón, ¿dónde hay un banco por aquí?** perdōn' ¿dōn'de ī o͞on bäng'kō pōr äkē'?

INFO You can find the best exchange rates at a bank; hotels, shops and currency exchange offices charge higher fees. Credit cards and traveler's checks are widely accepted.

Where can I change money? — **¿Dónde se puede cambiar dinero?** ¿dōn'de se po͞o·e'de kämbyär' dēne'rō?

What's the exchange rate today? — **¿Cómo está hoy el cambio?** ¿kō'mō estä' oy el käm'byō?

What's the commission charge?	**¿Cuánto cobra de comisión?** ¿kōō·än'tō kō'brä de kōmēsyōn'?
What time does the bank close?	**¿Hasta cuándo está abierto el banco?** ¿äs'tä kōō·än'dō estä' äbyer'tō el bäng'kō?
I'd like to change … dollars.	**Quisiera cambiar … dólares.** kēsye'rä kämbyär' … dō'läres.
I've wired for some money in my name. Has it arrived yet?	**He ordenado un giro telegráfico a mi nombre. ¿Ha llegado ya?** e ōrdenä'dō ōōn he'rō telegrä'fēkō ä mē nōm'bre. ¿ä lyegä'dō yä?
Can I use my credit card to get cash?	**¿Puedo sacar dinero con mi tarjeta de crédito?** ¿pōō·e'dō säkär' dēne'rō kōn mē tärhe'tä de kre'dētō?
I'd like to withdraw some money from my bank account.	**Quisiera retirar dinero de mi cuenta bancaria.** kēsye'rä retērär' dēne'rō de mē kōō·en'tä bängkä'rya.
I'd like to cash a traveller's check.	**Quisiera cobrar un cheque de viaje.** kēsye'rä kōbrär' ōōn tshe'ke de vyä'he.
What's the maximum I can withdraw?	**¿Cuál es el importe máximo que se puede retirar?** ¿kōō·äl' es el ēmpōr'te mä'ksēmō ke se pōō·e'de retērär'?

? **¿Cómo desea el dinero?** ¿kō'mō dese'ä el dēne'rō? — How would you like it?

In small bills, please.	**En billetes pequeños, por favor.** en bēlye'tes peke'nyōs, pōr fävōr'.

Money Matters

amount	**el importe** el ēmpōr'te
ATM	**el cajero automático** el kähe'rō outōmä'tēkō
bank	**el banco** el bäng'kō
bank account	**la cuenta bancaria** lä kōō·en'tä bäng·kar'yä
bill	**el billete** el bēlye'te
cash	**el dinero al contado** el dēne'rō äl kōntä'dō
in -	**en efectivo** en efektē'vō
cashier's counter	**la caja** lä kä'hä
change	**el cambio** el käm'byō
to change	**cambiar** kämbyär'
check	**el cheque** el tshe'ke
coin	**la moneda** lä mōne'dä
commission	**la comisión** lä kōmēsyōn'
counter	**la ventanilla** lä ventänē'lyä
credit card	**la tarjeta de crédito** lä tärhe'tä de kre'dētō
currency exchange office	**la casa de cambio** lä kä'sä de käm'byō
maximum amount	**el importe máximo** el ēmpōr'te mä'ksēmō
money	**el dinero** el dēne'rō
to pay in cash	**pagar al contado** pägär' äl kōntä'dō

8

payment	**el pago** el pä'gō
percent	**por ciento** pōr syen'tō
receipt	**el recibo** el resē'bō
savings book	**la libreta de ahorros** lä lēbre'tä de ä·ō'rrōs
signature	**la firma** lä fēr'mä
transfer	**la transferencia** lä tränferen'syä
traveler's check	**el cheque de viaje** el tshe'ke de vyä'he
to withdraw money	**retirar dinero** retērär' dēne'rō

INTERNET

Where's an internet café around here?	**¿Dónde hay un cibercafé por aquí?** ¿dōn'de ī o͞on sēberkäfe' por äkē?
I'd like to send an e-mail.	**Quisiera enviar un correo ⟨Sp: un mensaje⟩.** ¿kēsye'rä envēär' o͞on kōre'o ⟨Sp: un mensahe⟩.
Which computer can I use?	**¿Qué computadora ⟨Sp: ordenador⟩ puedo usar?** ¿kē kōmpo͞otädō'rä ⟨Sp: ōrdenädōr'⟩ po͞o·e'dō o͞osär?
How much is it for 15 minutes?	**¿Cuánto cuesta el cuarto de hora?** ¿ko͞o·än'to ko͞o·es'tä el ko͞o·ä'tro de ō'rä?
Could you help me, please?	**¿Puede ayudarme, por favor?** ¿po͞o·e'de äyo͞odär'me, pōr fävōr'?

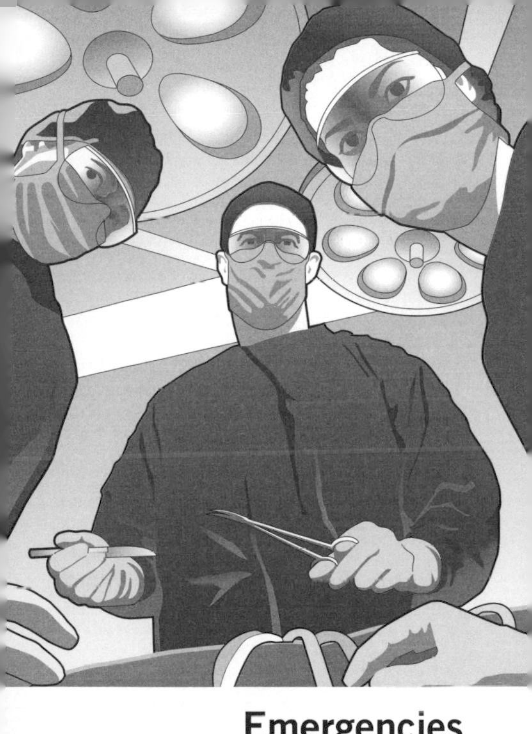

Emergencies

HEALTH

Information

Could you recommend a general practitioner? **¿Puede recomendarme un médico de medicina general?** ¿pōō·e'de rekōmendär'me ōōn me'dēkōde medēsē'nä heneräl?

Does *he/she* speak English? **¿Habla inglés?** ¿ä'blä ēng·gles'?

What are *his/her* office hours? **¿Cuándo tiene horas de consulta?** ¿kōō·än'dōtye'ne ō'räs de kōnsōōl'tä?

INFO For a trip to Latin America you should make sure you have adequate health insurance. If you suffer from any permanent medical conditions, be sure you bring enough medication with you to last the whole trip. Take care at high altitudes until you are acclimatized.

My *husband/wife* is sick. **Mi *esposo/esposa* está ♂ enfermo/ ♀ enferma.** mē *espō'sō/espō'sä* estä' ♂ enfer'mō/♀ enfer'mä.

Please call *an ambulance/a doctor*! **Por favor, ¡llame *una ambulancia/ a un médico de urgencia*!** pōr fävōr', ¡lyä'me *ōō'nä ämbōōlän'syä/ä ōōn me'dēkōde ōōrhen'syä*!

Where are you taking *him/her*? **¿Adónde *le/la* va a llevar?** ¿ädōn'de *le/lä* vä ä lyevär?

I'd like to stay with *him/her.*	**Quiero ♂ acompañarle / ♀ acompañarla.** kye'rō ♂ äkōmpänyär'le / ♀ äkōmpänyär'lä.
Where's the nearest (24-hour) pharmacy?	**¿Dónde está la farmacia (de guardia) más próxima?** ¿dōn'de estä' lä färmä'syä (de gōō·är'dyä) mäs prō'ksēmä?

Drugstore

Do you have anything for...?	**¿Tienen algo contra...?** ¿tye'nen äl'gōkōn'trä...?
How should it be taken?	**¿Cómo se debe tomar?** ¿kō'mōse de'be tōmär'?
I need this medicine.	**Necesito este medicamento.** nesesē'tōes'te medēkämen'tō.

! **Este medicamento necesita receta médica.** es'te medēkämen'tōnesesē'tä rese'tä me'dēkä. — You need a prescription for this medicine.

! **No lo tenemos aquí.** nōlōtene'mōs äkē'. — We don't have that.

When can I get it?	**¿Cuándo lo puedo tener?** ¿kōō·än'dōlōpōō·e'dōtener'?

9

Instructions

antes de las comidas än'tes de läs kōmē'däs	before meals
dejar disolver en la boca de<u>h</u>är' dēsolver' en lä bō'kä	allow to dissolve in the mouth
después de las comidas despōō·es' de läs kōmē'däs	after meals
efectos secundarios efek'tōs sekōōndär'yōs	side effects
en ayunas en äyōō'näs	on an empty stomach
para uso externo pä'rä ōō'sōekster'nō	for external use
para uso rectal pä'rä ōō'sōrektäl'	for rectal use
sin masticar sēn mästēkär'	whole, unchewed
tres veces al día tres ve'ses äl dē'ä	three times a day

Drugstores

antiseptic ointment	**el ungüento antiséptico** el ōōngōō·en'tōäntēsep'tēkō
antibiotic	**el antibiótico** el äntēbē·ō'tēkō
anti-itch cream	**la pomada contra el picor** lä pōmä'dä kōn'trä el pēkōr'
antiseptic solution	**el desinfectante** el desēnfektän'te
aspirin	**la aspirina** lä äspērē'nä
Band-Aid ®	**las vendas *f/pl*** läs ven'däs
charcoal tablets	**las pastillas de carbón *f/pl*** läs pästē'lyäs de kärbōn'

circulatory stimulant	**el remedio circulatorio** el reme'dyōsērkōōlätōr'yō
condom	**el condón** el kōndōn'
contraceptive pills	**las píldoras anticonceptivas** ***f/pl*** läs pēl'dōräs äntēkōnseptē'väs
cotton	**el algodón** el älgōdōn'
cough syrup	**el jarabe para la tos** el härä'be pä'rä lä tōs
drops	**las gotas** ***f/pl*** läs gō'täs
drugstore	**la farmacia** lä färmä'syä
elastic bandage	**la venda elástica** lä ven'dä eläs'tēkä
first-aid kit	**el botiquín** el bōtēkēn'
gauze bandage	**la venda de gasa** lä ven'dä de gä'sä
information leaflet	**el prospecto** el prōspek'tō
injection	**la inyección** lä ēnyeksyōn'
insulin	**la insulina** lä ēnsōōlē'nä
iodine	**el yodo** el yō'dō
laxative	**el laxante** el läksän'te
fever-reducing medication	**el antipirético** el äntēpēre'tēkō
night duty	**el servicio nocturno** el servē'syōnōktōōr'nō
ointment	**la pomada** lä pōmä'dä
ointment for mosquito bites	**la pomada para las picaduras de mosquitos** lä pōmä'dä pä'rä läs pēkädōō'räs de mōskē'tōs
ointment for sun allergy	**la pomada para alergias solares** lä pōmä'dä pä'rä älerhē'äs sōlä'res

9

ointment for sunburn	**la pomada para quemaduras solares** lä pōmä'dä pä'rä kemädōō'räs sōlä'res
painkiller	**el analgésico** el änälhe'sēkō
peppermint tea	**la infusión de menta** lä ēnfōōsyōn' de men'tä
plaster	**el esparadrapo** el espärädrä'pō
prescription	**la receta** lä rese'tä
sanitary napkin	**las toallas sanitarias *f/pl* 〈Sp: las compresas *f/pl*〉** läs tō·ä'lyäs sänētär'yäs 〈Sp: läs kōmpre'säs〉
sleeping pills	**el somnífero** el sōmnē'ferō
something for…	**el medicamento contra…** el medēkämen'tōkōn'trä…
with prescription	**con receta** kōn rese'tä

➡ *See also: word list Diseases, Doctor, Hospital (p. 216)*

suppository	**el supositorio** el sōōpōsētōr'yō
tablets	**los comprimidos *m/pl*** lōs kōmprēmē'dōs
tampons	**los tampones *m/pl*** lōs tämpō'nes
thermometer	**el termómetro** el termō'metrō
tranquilizer	**el tranquilizante** el trang·kēlēsän'te

➡ *See also: word list Diseases, Doctor, Hospital (p. 216)*

At the Doctor's

I have a (bad) cold.	**Estoy (muy) ♂ resfriado / ♀ resfriada.** estoi' (mōō'ē) ♂ resfrē·ä'dō / ♀ resfrē·ädä.

I have …	**Tengo …** teng'gō …
diarrhea.	**diarrea.** dē·äre'ä.
a (high) fever.	**fiebre (alta).** fye'bre (äl'tä).
constipation.	**estreñimiento.** estrenyēmyen'to.
My … *hurts/hurt.*	**Me *duele/duelen* …** me *dōō·e'le/dōō·e'len* …

➡ *See also: word list Parts of the Body and Organs (p. 214)*

I have pains here.	**Tengo dolores aquí.** teng'gōdōlō'res äkē'.
I've vomited (several times).	**He vomitado (varias veces).** e vōmētä'dō(vär'yäs ve'ses).
My stomach is upset.	**Tengo una indigestión.** teng'gōōō'nä ēndēhestyōn'.
I can't move …	**No puedo mover …** nōpōō·e'dōmōver' …

➡ *See also: word list Parts of the Body and Organs (p. 214)*

I hurt myself.	**Me he herido.** me e erē'dō.
I fell.	**Me he caído.** me e kä·ē'dō.
I've been *stung/ bitten* by …	**Me ha *picado/mordido* …** me ä *pēkä'dō / mōrdē'dō* …

9

What you should tell the doctor

I have (not) been vaccinated against …	**(No) He sido ♂ vacunado/♀ vacunada contra …** (nō) e sē'dō♂ väkōōnä'dō/ ♀ väkōōnä'dä kōn'trä …
My last tetanus shot was about … years ago.	**Mi última vacuna contra el tétano fue hace … años.** mē ōōl'tēmä väkōō'nä kōn'trä el te'tänōfōō·e' ä'se … ä'nyōs.
I'm allergic to penicillin.	**Soy ♂ alérgico/♀ alérgica a la penicilina.** soi ♂ äler'h̲ēkō/ ♀ äler'h̲ēkä ä lä penēsēlē'nä.
I have …	**Tengo …** teng'gō…
high/*low* blood pressure.	**la tensión *alta*/*baja*.** lä tensyōn' *äl'tä*/*bä'h̲ä*.
a pacemaker.	**un marcapasos.** ōōn märkäpä'sōs.
I'm … months pregnant.	**Estoy embarazada de … meses.** estoi' embäräsä'dä de … me'ses.
I'm diabetic	**Soy ♂ diabético/♀ diabética.** soi ♂ dē·äbe'tēkō/ ♀ dē·äbe'tēkä.
I'm HIV-positive.	**Soy VIH ♂ positivo/♀ positiva.** soi ōō've-ē-ä'tshe ♂ pōsētē'vō/ ♀ pōsētē'vä.
I take this medicine regularly.	**Tomo estos medicamentos con regularidad.** tō'mōes'tōs medēkämen'tōs kōn regōōlärēdäd'.

What the doctor says

¿Qué molestias tiene? ¿ke mōles'tyäs tye'ne?	What's the problem?
¿Dónde le duele? ¿dōn'de le dōō·e'le?	Where does it hurt?
Abra la boca. ä'brä lä bō'kä.	Open your mouth, please.
Saque la lengua. sä'ke lä leng'gōō·ä.	Show me your tongue, please.
Tosa. tō'sä.	Cough.
Por favor, desnúdese. pōr fävōr', desnōō'dese.	Get undressed, please.
Por favor, remánguese. pōr fävōr', remäng'gese.	Roll up your sleeve, please.
Respire hondo. Mantenga la respiración. respē're ōn'dō. mänteng'gä lä resperäsyōn'.	Breathe deeply. Hold your breath.
¿Desde cuándo tiene esas molestias? ¿dez'de kōō·än'dōtye'ne e'säs mōles'tyäs?	How long have you felt this way?
¿Está ♂ vacunado/♀ vacunada contra ...? ¿esta' ♂ väkōōnä'dō/ ♀ väkōōnä'dä kōn'trä ...?	Have you been vaccinated against ...?
Tenemos que hacerle radiografías. tene'mōs ke äser'le rädyōgräfē'äs.	We need to take some X-rays.

9

... está ♂ roto/♀ rota. ... estä' ♂ rō'tō/♀ rō'tä.	... is broken.
... está ♂ dislocado/♀ dislocada. ... es'tä ♂ dēslōkä'dō/♀ dēslōkä'dä.	... is sprained.
Tenemos que hacerle un análisis de *sangre/orina.* tene'mōs ke äser'le o͞on änä'lēsēs de *säng'gre/ōrē'nä.*	I need a *blood/urine* sample.
Hay que operarle. ī ke ōperär'le.	You'll have to have an operation.
Tengo que enviarle a un especialista. teng'gōke envē·är'le ä o͞on espesyälēs'tä.	I need to refer you to a specialist.
No es nada grave. nōes nä'dä grä'vc.	It's nothing serious.
Tome dos veces al día ... *comprimidos/gotas.* tō'me dōs ve'ses äl dē'ä ... *kōmprēmē'dōs/gō'täs.*	Take ... *tablets/drops* twice a day.
Vuelva *mañana/dentro de ... días.* vo͞o·el'vä *mänyä'nä/den'trōde ... dē'äs.*	Come back *tomorrow/ in ... days.*

Ask the doctor

Is it serious?	**¿Es grave?** ¿es grä've?
Can you give me a doctor's certificate?	**¿Puede usted darme un certificado médico?** ¿po͞o·e'do͞oste' där'me o͞on sertēfēkä'dōme'dēkō?
Do I have to come back?	**¿Tengo que volver otra vez?** ¿teng'gōke vōlver' ō'trä ves?

Could you give me a receipt in English for my medical insurance?	**¿Puede darme un recibo en inglés para mi seguro?** ¿po͞o·e'de där'me o͞on resē'bo͞en ēng·gles' pä'rä mē sego͞o'rō?

In the Hospital

Is there anyone here who speaks English?	**¿Hay alguien aquí que hable inglés?** ¿ī äl'gyen äkē, ke ä'ble ēng·gles'?
I'd like to speak to a doctor.	**Quisiera hablar con un médico.** kēsye'rä äblär' kōn o͞on me'dēkō.

➡ *See also: At the Doctor's (p. 208)*

What's the diagnosis?	**¿Cuál es el diagnóstico?** ¿ko͞o·äl' es el dē·ägnōs'tēkō?
I'd rather have the operation in the United States.	**Prefiero operarme en los Estados Unidos.** prefye'rōōperär'me en lōs estä'dōs o͞onē'dōs.
The insurance will pay my trip home.	**Tengo un seguro para la vuelta.** teng'gōo͞on sego͞o'rōpä'rä lä vo͞o·el'tä.
Would you please notify my family?	**Por favor, informe a mi familia.** pōr fävōr', ēnfōr'me ä mē fämē'lyä.
Can I have a private room?	**¿Podría tener una habitación individual?** ¿pōdrē'ä tener' o͞o'nä äbētäsyōn' ēndēvēdo͞o·äl'?
How long do I have to stay here?	**¿Hasta cuándo tengo que estar aquí?** ¿äs'tä ko͞o·än'dōteng'gōke estär' äkē'?

9

When can I get out of bed?	**¿Cuándo puedo levantarme?** ¿ko͞o·än'dōpo͞o·e'dōleväntär'me?
Could you give me something *for pain/ to get to sleep*?	**Por favor, déme algo *contra los dolores/para dormir.*** pōr fävōr', de'me äl'gō*kōn' trä lōs dōlō' res/pä' rä dōrmēr'*.
I'd like to be discharged (at my own risk).	**Por favor, déme el alta (bajo mi responsabilidad).** pōr fävōr', de'me el äl'tä (bä'h̲ōmē respōnsäbēlēdäd').
Please give me a certificate stating my length of stay.	**Por favor, déme un certificado con la duración de mi estancia.** pōr fävōr', de'me o͞on sertēfēkä'dōkōn lä do͞oräsyōn' de mē estän'syä.

Parts of the Body and Organs

abdomen	**el vientre** el vyen'tre
ankle	**el tobillo** el tōbē'lyō
appendix	**el apéndice** el äpen'dēse
arm	**el brazo** el brä'sō
back	**la espalda** lä espäl'dä
bladder	**la vejiga** lä veh̲ē'gä
body	**el cuerpo** el ko͞o·er'pō
bone	**el hueso** el o͞o·e'sō
breasts	**los senos** lōs se'nōs
bronchial tubes	**los bronquios** ***m/pl*** lōs brōng'kyōs
chest	**el pecho** el pe'tshō
disk	**el disco intervertebral** el dēs'kōentervertebräl'
ear	**el oído** el ō·ē'dō

eardrum	**el tímpano** el tēm'pänō
eye	**el ojo** el ō'h̲ō
finger	**el dedo** el de'dō
foot	**el pie** el pye'
forehead	**la frente** lä fren'te
gall bladder	**la vesícula biliar** lä vesē'ko͞olä bēlēär'
hand	**la mano** lä mä'nō
head	**la cabeza** lä käbe'sä
heart	**el corazón** el köräsōn'
hip	**la cadera** lä käde'rä
intestine	**el intestino** el ēntestē'nō
kidney	**el riñón** el rēnyōn'
knee	**la rodilla** lä rōdē'lyä
kneecap	**la rótula** lä rō'to͞olä
leg	**la pierna** lä pyer'nä
liver	**el hígado** el ē'gädō
lung	**el pulmón** el po͞olmōn'
mouth	**la boca** lä bō'kä
muscle	**el músculo** el mo͞os'ko͞olō
neck	**la nuca** lä no͞o'kä
nerve	**el nervio** el ner'vyō
nose	**la nariz** lä närēs'
penis	**el pene** el pe'ne
rib	**la costilla** lä kōstē'lyä
rib cage	**el tórax** el tō'räks
shin (bone)	**la tibia** lä tē'byä
shoulder	**el hombro** el ōm'brō
shoulder blade	**el omóplato** el ōmō'plätō
sinus	**el seno frontal** el se'nōfrōntäl'

skin	**la piel** lä pyel'
spine	**la columna vertebral** lä kōlo͞om'nä vertebräl'
stomach	**el estómago** el estō'mägō
tendon	**el tendón** el tendōn'
thigh	**el muslo** el mo͞os'lō
throat	**la garganta** lä gärgän'tä
thyroid (gland)	**el tiroides** el tēroi'des
toe	**el dedo del pie** el de'dōdel pye'
tongue	**la lengua** lä leng'go͞o·ä
tonsils	**las amígdalas *f/pl*** läs ämēg'däläs
tooth	**el diente** el dyen'te
vagina	**la vagina** lä väh̲ē'nä

Diseases, Doctor, Hospital

abscess	**el absceso** el äbse'sō
AIDS	**el sida** el sē'dä
allergy	**la alergia** lä äler'h̲ē·ä
appendicitis	**la apendicitis** lä äpendēsē'tēs
asthma	**el asma** el äz'mä
insect bite	**la picadura** lä pēkädo͞o'rä
bleeding	**la hemorragia** lä emōrä'h̲ē·ä
blister	**la ampolla** lä ämpō'lyä
blood poisoning	**la intoxicación de la sangre** lä ēntōksēkäsyōn' de lä säng'gre
blood pressure	**la tensión** lä tensyōn'
blood transfusion	**la transfusión de sangre** lä tränsfo͞osyōn' de säng'gre

blood type	**el grupo sanguíneo** el gro͞o'pōsäng·gē'ne·ō
broken	**roto** rō'tō
bruise	**la contusión** lä kōntōōsyōn'
burn	**la quemadura** lä kemädo͞o'rä
cardiac infarction	**el infarto** el ēnfär'tō
certificate	**el certificado médico** el sertēfēkä'dōme'dēkō
chicken pox	**la varicela** lä värēse'lä
chills	**los escalofríos** ***m/pl*** lōs eskälōfrē'ōs
circulatory problems	**los trastornos circulatorios** ***m/pl*** lōs trästōr'nōs sērko͞olätōr'yōs
cold	**el resfrío ⟨Sp: el constipado⟩** el resfrē'ō⟨Sp: el kōnstēpä'dō⟩
colic	**el cólico** el kō'lēkō
concussion	**la conmoción cerebral** lä kōnmōsyōn' serebräl'
conjunctivitis	**la conjuntivitis** lä kōnh͟o͞ontēvē'tēs
constipation	**el estreñimiento** el estrenyēmyen'tō
cough	**la tos** lä tōs
cystitis	**la cistitis** lä sēstē'tēs
diarrhea	**la diarrea** lä dē·äre'ä
dizziness	**el mareo** el märe'ō
doctor *m*	**el médico** el me'dēkō
doctor *f*	**la medica** lä me'dēkä
fainted	**desmayado** desmäyä'dō
fever	**la fiebre ⟨Mex. la calentura⟩** lä fye'bre ⟨Mex: lä kälento͞o'rä⟩
flu	**la gripe** lä grē'pe

food poisoning	**la intoxicación alimenticia** lä ēntōksēkäsyōn' älēmentē'syä
fungal infection	**la micosis** lä mēkō'sēs
gallstones	**los cálculos** ***m/pl*** **biliares** lōs käl'ko͞olōs bēlē·ä'res
general practitioner	**el médico de medicina general** el me'dēkōde medēsē'nä h̲eneräl'
German measles	**la rubéola** lä ro͞obe'ōlä
gynecologist *m*	**el ginecólogo** el h̲ēnekō'lōgō
gynecologist *f*	**la ginecóloga** lä h̲ēnekō'lōgä
hay fever	**la fiebre del heno** lä fey'bre del e'nō
headache	**el dolor de cabeza** el dōlōr' de käbe'sä
heart	**el corazón** el kōräsōn'
heart attack	**el ataque cardíaco** el ätä'ke kärdē'äkō
hernia	**la hernia inguinal** lä er'nyä ēngēnäl'
herpes	**el herpes** el er'pes
high blood pressure	**la tensión alta** lä tensyōn' äl'tä
infection	**la infección** lä ēnfeksyōn'
infectious	**contagioso** kōntäh̲ē·ō'sō
inflammation	**la inflamación** lä ēnflämäsyōn'
kidney stones	**los cálculos renales** ***m/pl*** lōs käl'ko͞olos renä'les
low blood pressure	**la tensión baja** lä tensyon' bä'h̲ä
lumbago	**el lumbago** el lo͞ombä'gō
malaria	**la malaria** lä mälä'ryä
measles	**el sarampión** el särämpyōn'
middle-ear infection	**la otitis media** lä ōtē'tēs me'dyä
migraine	**la jaqueca** lä h̲äke'kä
mumps	**las paperas** ***f/pl*** läs päpe'räs

nausea	**las náuseas** ***f/pl*** läs nou'se·äs
nurse	**la enfermera** lä enferme'rä
office hours	**las horas** ***f/pl*** **de consulta** läs ō'räs de kōnso͞ol'tä
to operate	**operar** ōperär'
ophthalmologist	**el oculista** el ōko͞olēs'tä
pacemaker	**el marcapasos** el märkäpä'sōs
pain(s)	**los dolores** ***m/pl*** lōs dōlō'res
pediatrician	**el pediatra** el pedē'äträ
pneumonia	**la pulmonía** lä po͞olmōnē'ä
polio	**la parálisis infantil** lä pärä'lēsēs ēnfäntēl'
pregnant	**embarazada** embäräsä'dä
to prescribe	**recetar** resetär'
sprain	**la distorsión** lä dēstōrsyōn'
rash	**la erupción** ⟨**Mex: el salpullido**⟩ lä ero͞opsyōn' ⟨Mex: el sälpo͞olyē'dō⟩
rheumatism	**el reuma** el re'o͞omä
scarlet fever	**la escarlatina** lä eskärlätē'nä
sexually transmitted disease	**la enfermedad venérea** lä enfermedäd' vene're·ä
shock	**el shock** el shōk
snake bite	**la mordedura de culebra** lä mōrdedo͞o'rä de ko͞ole'brä
sore throat	**el dolor de garganta** el dōlōr' de gärgän'tä
sprained	**distorsionado** dēstōrsyōnä'dō
sprained tendon	**la distorsión de un tendón** lä dēstōrsyōn' de o͞on tendōn'

stomach ache	**el dolor de estómago** el dōlōr' de estō'mägō
stomach ulcer	**la úlcera de estómago** lä o͞ol'serä de estō'mägō
stroke	**la apoplejía** lä äpōplehē'ä
sunburn	**la quemadura del sol** lä kemädo͞o'rä del sōl'
sunstroke	**la insolación** lä ēnsōläsyōn'
swelling	**la hinchazón** lä ēntshäsōn'
tetanus	**el tétano** el te'tänō
tonsillitis	**la amigdalitis** lä ämēgdälē'tēs
torn ligament	**la rotura de ligamento** lä rōto͞o'rä de lēgämen'tō
typhus	**el tifus** el tē'fo͞os
ulcer	**la úlcera** lä o͞ol'serä
urine analysis	**el análisis de orina** el änä'lēsēs de ōrē'nä
vaccination	**la vacunación** lä väko͞onäsyōn'
vaccination certificate	**el certificado de vacunación** el sertēfēkä'dōde väko͞onäsyōn'
to vomit	**vomitar** vōmētär'
whooping cough	**la tos convulsa ⟨Sp: ferina⟩** lä tōs kōnvo͞ol'sä ⟨Sp: ferē'nä⟩
to X-ray	**radiografiar** rädyōgräfēär'

At the Dentist's

This tooth … hurts.	**Este diente … me duele.** es'te dyen'te … me dōō·e'le.
here	**de aquí** de äkē'
back here	**de detrás** de deträs'
on the left	**de la izquierda** de lä ēskyer'dä
on the top	**de arriba** de ärē'bä
on the right	**de la derecha** de lä dere'tshä
on the bottom	**de abajo** de äbä'ẖō
in front	**de delante** de delän'te
This tooth has broken off.	**El diente está roto.** el dyen'te estä' rō'tō.
I've lost a filling.	**He perdido una tapadura 〈Sp: un empaste〉.** e perdē'dōōō'nä täpädōō'rä 〈Sp: oon empäs'te〉.
Can you do a temporary job on the tooth?	**¿Puede usted tratarme provisionalmente este diente?** ¿pōō·e'de ōōste' trätär'me prōvēsyōnälmen'te es'te dyen'te?
Please don't pull the tooth.	**Por favor, no extraiga el diente.** pōr fävōr', nōekstrī'gä el dyen'te.
Would you give me an injection, please.	**Por favor, póngame una inyección.** pōr fävōr', pōng'gäme ōō'nä ēnyeksyōn'.
I'd rather not have an injection, please.	**Por favor, no me ponga ninguna inyección.** pōr fävōr', nōme pōng'gä nēng·gōō'nä enyeksyōn.

9

What the dentist says

Necesita ... nesesē'tä ...	You need ...
un puente. ōōn pōō·en'te.	a bridge.
una tapadura ⟨Sp: un empaste⟩. ōō'nä täpädōō'rä ⟨Sp: ōōn empäs'te⟩.	a filling.
una corona. ōō'nä kōrō'nä.	a crown.
Tengo que extraerle el diente. teng'gōke eksträ·er'le el dyen'te.	I'll have to pull the tooth.
Por favor, enjuagar bien. pōr fävōr', enhōō·ägär' byen'.	Rinse out your mouth, please.
Por favor, no comer nada por dos horas. pōr fävōr', nōkōmer' nä'dä pōr dōs ō'räs.	Please don't eat for two hours.

At the Dentist's

abscess	**el absceso** el äbse'sō
anesthetic	**la anestesia** lä äneste'syä
braces	**el aparato dental** el äpärä'tōdentäl'
bridge	**el puente** el pōō·en'te
crown	**la corona** lä kōrō'nä
dental clinic	**la clínica dental** lä klē'nēkä dentäl'
dentist	**el dentista** el dentēs'tä
dentures *(false teeth)*	**la dentadura postiza** lä dentädōō'rä pōstē'sä
filling	**la tapadura ⟨Sp: el empaste⟩** lä täpädōō'rä ⟨Sp: el empas'te⟩
gold crown	**la corona de oro** lä kōrō'nä de ō'rō

gums	**las encías** ***f/pl*** läs ensē'äs
hole	**el agujero** el ägo͞oh̲e'rō
infection	**la infección** lä ēnfeksyōn'
injection	**la inyección** lä ēnyeksyōn'
jaw	**la mandíbula** lä mändē'bo͞olä
molar	**la muela** lä mo͞o·e'lä
mold	**el molde** el mōl'de
nerve	**el nervio** el ner'vyō
office hours	**la hora de consulta** lä ō'rä de kōnso͞ol'tä
pivot tooth	**el diente de espiga** el dyen'te de espē'gä
porcelain crown	**la corona de porcelana** lä kōrō'nä de pōrselä'nä
root	**la raíz** lä rä·ēs'
root canal work	**el tratamiento de la raíz** el trätämyen'tōde lä rä·ēs'
tartar	**el sarro** el sä'rō
temporary filling	**el arreglo provisional** el äre'glōprōvēsyōnäl'
to extract	**extraer** eksträ·er'
tooth	**el diente** el dyen'te
tooth decay	**la caries** lä kär'yes
wisdom tooth	**la muela del juicio** lä mo͞o·e'lä del h̲o͞o·ē'syō

POLICE; LOST AND FOUND

Where is the nearest police station?	**¿Dónde está la estación de policía ⟨Sp: la comisaría⟩ más cercana?** ¿dōn'de estä' lä estäsyōn' de pōlēsē'ä ⟨Sp: lä kōmēsärē'ä⟩ mäs serkä'nä?
Does anyone here speak English?	**¿Hay alguien aquí que hable inglés?** ¿ī äl'gyen äkē' ke ä'ble ēng·gles'?
I'd like to report…	**Quiero denunciar …** kye'rōdeno͞onsyär' …
a theft.	**un robo.** o͞on rō'bō.
a mugging.	**un atraco.** o͞on äträ'kō.
an accident	**un accidente.** o͞on äksēden'te.
a rape.	**una violación.** o͞o'nä vē·ōläsyōn'.
My *daughter/son* has disappeared.	**Mi *hija/hijo* ha desaparecido.** mē *ē'h̲ä/ē'h̲ōä* desäpäresē'dō.
My … has been stolen.	**Me han robado …** me än rōbä'dō…
I've lost…	**He perdido …** e perdē'dō…
My house has been broken into.	**Me han forzado la casa.** me än fōrsä'dōlä kä'sä.
I need a copy of the official report for insurance purposes.	**Necesito un certificado para mi seguro.** nesesē'tōo͞on sertēfēkä'dō pä'rä mē sego͞o'rō.
I'd like to speak to my *lawyer/consulate.*	**Quiero hablar con *mi abogado/ el consulado.*** kye'rōä'blär kōn mē *äbōgä'dō/el kōnso͞olä'dō.*

What the police say

Rellene este formulario, por favor. relye'ne es'te fōrmo͞olär'yō, pōr fävōr'.	Please fill out this form.
Su pasaporte, por favor. so͞o päsäpōr'te, pōr favōr'.	Your passport, please.
¿Dónde vive usted ***en los Estados Unidos / aquí*****?** ¿dōn'de vē've o͞oste' en *lōs estä'dōs o͞onē'dōs / äkē'* ?	What is your address *in the United States / here*?
¿***Cuándo / Dónde*** **ha pasado?** ¿*'ko͞o·än'dō / dōn'de* ä päsä'dō?	*When / Where* did this happen?
Por favor, diríjase al consulado de su país. pōr fävōr', dērē'h̲äse äl kōnso͞olä'dōde so͞o pä·ēs'.	Please get in touch with your consulate.

Police; Lost and Found

accident	**el accidente** el äksēden'te
to arrest	**detener** detener'
to break into	**forzar** fōrsär'
car	**el carro ⟨Sp: el coche⟩** el kä'rō⟨Sp: el kō'tshe⟩
car keys	**las llaves del carro ⟨Sp: coche⟩ *f/pl*** läs lyä'ves del kä'rō ⟨Sp. kō'tshe⟩
car radio	**la radio del coche** lä rä'dyōdel kō'tshe
car registration papers	**la documentación del coche** lä dōko͞omentäsyōn' del kō'tshe
consulate	**el consulado** el kōnso͞olä'dō
drug smuggling	**el narcotráfico** el närkōträ'fēkō

drugs	**las drogas** ***f/pl*** läs drō'gäs
form	**el formulario** el fōrmo͞olär'yō
ID	**la tarjeta ⟨Sp: el carnet⟩ de identidad** lä tärhe'tä ⟨Sp: el kärnet'⟩ de ēdentēdäd'
lawyer	**el abogado** el äbōgä'dō
lost	**perdido** perdē'dō
lost and found bureau	**la oficina de objetos perdidos** lä ōfēsē'nä de ōbhe'tōs perdē'dōs
to molest	**abusar** äbo͞osär'
passport	**el pasaporte** el päsäpōr'te
police	**la policía** lä pōlēsē'ä
police station	**la estación de policía ⟨Sp: la comisaría⟩** lä estäsyōn' de pōlēsē'ä ⟨Sp: lä kōmēsärē'ä⟩
policeman	**el policía** el pōlēsē'ä
policewoman	**la policía** lä pōlēsē'ä
purse	**la bolsa ⟨Sp: el bolso⟩** lä bōl'sä ⟨Sp: el bōl'sō⟩
rape	**la violación** lä vē·ōläsyōn'
report *(to police)*	**la denuncia** lä deno͞on'syä
robbery	**el atraco** el äträ'kō
smuggling	**el contrabando** el kōnträbän'dō
stolen	**robado** rōbä'dō
theft	**el robo** el rō'bō
thief	**el ladrón** el lädrōn'
wallet	**el monedero** el mōnede'rō
witness	**el testigo** el testē'gō

Time and Weather

TIME

Time of day

What time is it? **¿Qué hora es?** ¿ke ō'rä es?

INFO The numbers 1–12 are usually used for telling the time. For further clarification you can add **de la mañana** (am), **de la tarde** (pm), or for later in the evening **de la noche**. The twenty-four hour clock is also used, especially in written Spanish.

It's one o'clock. **Es la una.** es lä o͞o'nä.

It's two o'clock. **Son las dos.** sōn läs dōs.

It's quarter past five. **Son las cinco y cuarto.** sōn läs sēng'kō ē ko͞o·är'tō.

It's six-thirty. **Son las seis y media.** sōn läs se'ēs ē me'dyä.

It's quarter to nine. **Son las nueve menos cuarto.** sōn läs no͞o·e've me'nōs ko͞o·är'tō.

It's five after four. **Son las cuatro y cinco.** sōn läs ko͞o·ä'trō ē sēng'kō.

It's ten to eight. **Son las ocho menos diez.** sōn läs ō'tshō me'nōs dyes'.

(At) What time? **¿A qué hora?** ¿ä ke ō'rä?

At ten o'clock. **A las diez.** ä läs dyes'.

At about eleven.	**A las once aproximadamente.** ä läs ōn'se äprōksēmädämen'te.
At nine thirty sharp.	**A las nueve y media en punto.** ä läs noo͞'e've ē me'dyä en poo͞n'tō.
By four.	**Hasta las cuatro.** äs'tä läs koo͞'ä'trō.
From eight to nine (o'clock).	**De ocho a nueve.** de ō'tshō ä noo͞'e've.
Between ten and twelve (*noon/midnight*).	**Entre las diez y las doce (*de mediodía/de medianoche*)** en'tre läs dyes' ē läs dō'se (*de medyōdē'ä/de me'dyänō'tshe*).
In half an hour.	**Dentro de media hora.** den'trō de me'dyä ō'rä.
It's (too) late.	**Es (demasiado) tarde.** es (demäsyä'dō) tär'de.
It's still too early.	**Es aún temprano.** es ä·oo͞n' temprä'nō.

Basic Vocabulary

ago	**hace** ä'se
at night	**por la noche** pōr lä nō'tshe
at noon	**a mediodía** ä medyōdē'ä
before	**antes** än'tes
day	**el día** el dē'ä
day after tomorrow	**pasado mañana** päsä'dō mänyä'nä
day before yesterday	**anteayer** änte·äyer'

10

during the day	**de día** de dē'ä
earlier	**más temprano** mäs temprä'nō
early	**temprano** temprä'nō
every	**cada** kä'dä
every day	**todos los días** tō'dōs lōs dē'äs
every hour	**cada hora** kä'dä ō'rä
every week	**cada semana** kä'dä semä'nä
for	**desde** dez'de
half an hour	**media hora** me'dyä ō'rä
hour	**la hora** lä ō'rä
in the afternoon	**por la tarde** pōr lä tär'de
in the (early) evening	**por la tarde** pōr lä tär'de
in the morning	**por la mañana** pōr lä mänyä'nä
in the mornings	**por las mañanas** pōr läs mänyä'näs
in two weeks	**dentro de quince días** den'trō de kēn'se dē'äs
in/*on* time	**a tiempo** ä tyem'pō
last year	**el año pasado** el ä'nyō päsä'dō
late	**tarde** tär'de
later	**más tarde** mäs tär'de
minute	**el minuto** el mēnōō'tō
month	**el mes** el mes
next year	**el próximo año** el prō'ksēmō ä'nyō
now	**ahora** ä·ō'rä
on the weekend	**el fin de semana** el fēn de semä'nä
quarter of an hour	**el cuatro de hora** el kōō·ä'trō de ō'rä
recently	**hace poco** ä'se pō'kō
second	**el segundo** el segōōn'dō
since	**desde** dez'de

six months	**medio año** me'dyō ä'nyō
sometimes	**a veces** ä ve'ses
soon	**pronto ⟨Mex: ahorita⟩** prōn'tō ⟨Mex: ä·ōrē'tä⟩
this evening	**esta tarde** es'tä tär'de
till	**hasta** äs'tä
time	**el tiempo** el tyem'pō
today	**hoy** oi
tomorrow	**mañana** mänyä'nä
tonight	**esta noche** es'tä nō'tshe
until	**hasta** äs'tä
week	**la semana** lä semä'nä
year	**el año** el ä'nyō
yesterday	**ayer** äyer'

Seasons

spring	**la primavera** lä prēmäve'rä
summer	**el verano** el verä'nō
fall	**el otoño** el ōtō'nyō
winter	**el invierno** el ēnvyer'nō

Legal Holidays

Mardi Gras	**Carnaval** kärnäväl'
Good Friday	**Viernes Santo** vyer'nes sän'tō
Easter	**Pascua (de Resurrección)** päs'ko͞o·ä (de reso͞oreksyōn')
Ascension Thursday	**Ascensión** äsensyōn'
Corpus Christi	**Día del Corpus** dē'ä del kōr'po͞os

10

Pentecost Sunday	**(Pascua de) Pentecostés** (päs'ko͞o·ä de) pentekōstes'
All Saint's	**Todos los Santos** tō'dōs lōs sän'tōs
Christmas Eve	**Nochebuena** nōtshebo͞o·e'nä
Christmas	**Navidad** nävēdäd'
New Year's Eve	**Año Viejo** ä'nyō vye'hō
New Year's Day	**Año Nuevo** ä'nyō no͞o·e'vō

INFO Apart from the above holidays, also note January 6th: **día de reyes** (the Epiphany); March 19th: San José, **día del padre** (Feast of St Joseph, Father's Day); **Semana Santa** (Holy Week); August 15th: **Asunción de María** (the Assumption); September 16th: Mexican Independence Day; October 12th: **día de la raza** ⟨Sp: **hispanidad**⟩ (Columbus Day), and December 12th: **Nuestra Señora de Guadalupe** (Feast of Our Lady of Guadalupe, patron saint of Mexico.)

THE DATE

What's today's date?	**¿A cuántos estamos?** ¿ä ko͞o·än'tōs estä'mōs?
Today is the 2nd of July.	**Hoy es el dos de julio.** oi es el dōs de ho͞o'lyō.
Until April 24th.	**Hasta el veinticuatro de abril.** äs'tä el ve·ēntēko͞o·ä'trō de äbrēl'.
We're leaving on August 29th.	**Nos marchamos el veintinueve de agosto.** nōs märtshä'mōs el ve·ēntēno͞o·e've de ägōs'tō.

Days of the Week

Monday	**el lunes** el lōō'nes
Tuesday	**el martes** el mär'tes
Wednesday	**el miércoles** el myer'kōles
Thursday	**el jueves** el h̲ōō·e'ves
Friday	**el viernes** el vyer'nes
Saturday	**el sábado** el sä'badō
Sunday	**el domingo** el dōmēng'gō

Months

January	**enero** ene'rō
February	**febrero** febre'rō
March	**marzo** mär'sō
April	**abril** äbrēl'
May	**mayo** mä'yō
June	**junio** h̲ōō'nyō
July	**julio** h̲ōō'lyō
August	**agosto** ägōs'tō
September	**septiembre** septyem'bre
October	**octubre** ōktōō'bre
November	**noviembre** nōvyem'bre
December	**diciembre** dēsyem'bre

THE WEATHER

What's the weather going to be like today?	**¿Qué tiempo hará hoy?** ¿ke tyem'pō ärä' oi?

10

It's going to be	**Hará ...** ärä'...
warm.	**calor.** kälōr'.
hot.	**mucho calor.** mōō'tshō kälōr'.
cold.	**frío.** frē'ō.
cool.	**fresco.** fres'kō.
muggy.	**bochornoso.** bōtshōr'nō'sō.
It's pretty windy.	**Hace bastante viento.** ä'se bästän'te vyen'tō.
It's stormy.	**Hay tormenta.** ī tōrmen'tä.
What's the temperature?	**¿A cuántos grados estamos?** ¿ä kōō·än'tōs grä'dōs estä'mōs?
It's ... degrees *above/ below* zero.	**Estamos a ... grados *sobre/ bajo* cero.** estä'mōs ä ... grä'dōs *sō'bre/ bä'ho* se'rō.
It looks like *rain/ a thunderstorm*	**Parece que va a *llover/ haber tormenta.*** päre'se ke vä ä *lyōver'/äber' tōrmen'tä.*

Weather

air	**el aire** el ī're
air pressure	**la presión atmosférica** lä presyōn' ätmōsfe'rēkä
barometric pressure	**la presión barométrica** lä presyōn' bärōme'trēkä
clear skies	**despejado** despehä'dō
climate	**el clima** el klē'mä

cloud **la nube** lä no͞o'be
cloudy **nublado** no͞oblä'dō
cold **frío** frē'ō
cool **fresco** fres'kō
damp **húmedo** o͞o'medō
dawn **el amanecer** el ämäneser'
degree **el grado** el grä'dō
drizzle **la llovizna** lä lyōvēz'nä
dry **seco** se'kō
dusk **el crepúsculo** el krepo͞os'ko͞olō
earthquake **el terremoto** el terremō'tō
fog **la niebla** lä nye'blä
frost **la helada** lä elä'dä
hail **el granizo** el gränē'sō
hazy **brumoso** bro͞omō'sō
heat **el calor** el kalor'
heat wave **la ola de calor** lä ō'lä de kälōr'
high-pressure area **el anticiclón** el äntēsēklōn'
hot **caluroso** kälo͞orō'sō
hurricane **el huracán** el o͞oräkän'
I'm *cold/hot.* **tengo *frío/calor*** teng'gō *frē'ō/kälōr'*
ice **el hielo** el ye'lō
it's freezing **hace un frío glacial** a'se o͞on frē'ō gläsyäl'
lightning **el relámpago** el reläm'pägō
low-pressure area **el ciclón** el sēklōn'
moon **la luna** lä lo͞o'nä
muggy **bochornoso** bōtshōrnō'sō
overcast **nublado** no͞oblä'dō

English	Spanish	Pronunciation
rain	**la lluvia**	lä lyo͞o'vyä
rainy	**lluvioso**	lyo͞ovyō'sō
shower	**el chubasco**	el tsho͞obäs'kō
snow	**la nieve**	lä nye've
star	**la estrella**	lä estre'lyä
storm	**la tormenta**	lä tōrmen'tä
stormy	**tempestuoso**	tempesto͞o·ō'sō
sun	**el sol**	el sōl
sunny	**soleado**	sōle·ä'dō
sunrise	**la salida del sol**	lä sälē'dä del sōl'
sunset	**la puesta del sol**	lä po͞o·es'tä del sōl'
temperature	**la temperatura**	lä temperäto͞o'rä
thaw	**el deshielo**	el desye'lō
thunder	**el trueno**	el tro͞o·e'nō
thunderstorm	**la tormenta tronada**	lä tōrmen'tä trōnä'dä
variable	**inestable**	ēnestä'ble
warm	**cálido**	kä'lēdō
weather	**el tiempo**	el tyem'pō
weather report	**el parte meteorológico**	el pär'te mete·ōrōlō'h̲ēkō
wet	**mojado**	mōh̲ä'dō
wind	**el viento**	el vyen'tō
windchill factor	**el efecto enfriador del viento**	el efek'tō enfrē·ädōr' del vyen'tō
windy	**ventoso**	ventō'sō

Grammar

ARTICLES

Spanish is one of the languages that have a "grammatical gender". Articles, nouns, adjectives, and pronouns are either "masculine" or "feminine", not only those for living things (and their natural gender) but also those for objects and ideas. For example, Spanish grammar treats "car" and "love" as masculine and "bed" and "republic" as feminine. This kind of distinction is arbitrary, and no one would think of regarding these objects or ideas as being male or female.

	Singular		Plural	
	♂	♀	♂	♀
definite article	**el coche** the car	**la casa** the house	**los coches** the cars	**las casas** the houses
indefinite article	**un coche** a car	**una casa** a house	**unos coches** (some) cars	**unas casas** (some) houses

There is a neuter form of the article: **lo**; it is used with the masculine singular form of an adjective to express an idea: **lo bueno** the good, **lo útil** what is useful.

El is combined with the preposition **a** (to, for, at) to form **al**, and with the preposition **de** (of, from, by) to form **del**: **Voy al teatro.** I'm going to the theater. **Vengo del cine.** I'm coming from the movies.

The definite article is used with titles: **el señor Gómez** Mr. Gómez; but in direct address it is omitted: **Buenas tardes, señora Martínez.** Good evening, Mrs. Martínez.

The indefinite article is not used before a noun of nationality, occupation, etc.: **Mi amigo es abogado.** My friend is a lawyer; but it is used when the noun is modified: **Mi hermano es un abogado excelente.** My brother is an excellent lawyer.

The indefinite article is also not used before **otro** (which therefore means both "other" and "another"): **Quisiera otro vaso de vino.** I'd like to have another glass of wine.

NOUNS

Nouns ending in **-a, -ad, -ud, -ión,** and **-umbre** are generally feminine: **la mesa** the table, **la lección** the lesson. Nouns ending in **-o, -aje,** and **-or** are generally masculine: **el libro** the book, **el viaje** the trip. Among the exceptions: **la mano** the hand, **la foto** the photograph, **la labor** the work; **el mapa** the map, **el día** the day, **el idioma** the language.

The plural is formed by adding **-s** to nouns ending in a vowel, and usually by adding **-es** to nouns ending in a consonant:

	Singular	Plural
♂	**el libro** the book **el tren** the train	**los libros** the books **los trenes** the trains
♀	**la cama** the bed **la pared** the wall	**las camas** the beds **las paredes** the walls

Nouns ending in **-s** do not change the plural when the final syllable is not stressed: **el paraguas** the umbrella, **los paraguas** the umbrellas; when the final syllable is stressed, **-es** is added: **el autobús** the bus, **los autobuses** the buses.

Nouns ending in **-z** form the plural by changing the **z** to **c** and adding **-es: el lápiz** the pencil, **los lápices** the pencils; **la voz** the voice, **las voces** the voices.

Many nouns for occupations distinguish between male and female by the article alone: **el dentista, la dentista** the dentist.

Feminine nouns with a stressed **a** or **ha** at the beginning take the masculine article in the singular: **el agua** water; **el hambre** hunger (the **h** is always mute).

ADJECTIVES AND ADVERBS

Adjectives

Adjectives agree in gender and number with the noun they modify.

Adjectives ending in **-o** become feminine by changing **-o** to **-a: pequeño → pequeña** small.

Adjectives of nationality ending in **-l, -s,** or **-z** and adjectives ending in **-or, -án** or **-ón** become feminine by adding **-a: español → española** Spanish; **conservador → conservadora** conservative.

Other adjectives that end in a consonant have the same form in the masculine and the feminine: **difícil** difficult, **feliz** happy, lucky.

Adjectives ending in a vowel form the plural by adding **-s: el coche pequeño** the small car, **los coches pequeños** the small cars; **la cama pequeña** the small bed, **las camas pequeñas** the small beds.

Adjectives ending in a consonant form the plural by adding **-es: la lección fácil** the easy lesson, **las lecciones fáciles** the easy lessons.

Adjectives ending in **-z** form the plural by changing the **z** to **c** and adding **-es: el niño feliz** the happy child, **los niños felices** the happy children.

Note that adjectives generally follow the noun.

When **bueno** (good) and **malo** (bad) – and certain other adjectives – are used before a masculine singular noun, they drop their final **-o; un buen/mal restaurante** a good/bad restaurant.

When **grande** (large, great) is used before a masculine or feminine singular noun, it drops **-de: un gran amigo** a great friend, **una gran ciudad** a big city.

Adverbs

Adverbs are generally formed by adding **-mente** to the feminine of the adjective:
claro → clara → claramente clear
rápido → rápida → rápidamente fast
fácil → fácil → fácilmente easy

Sale rápidamente del metro. He gets fast off the subway.

Among adverbs that are not derived from adjectives: **ahora** now, **aquí** here, **allí** there, **poco** little, few, **bastante** enough, rather.

Comparison

The comparative is formed by placing **más** (more) or **menos** (less) before the adjective; and the superlative of **más** is formed by adding the definite article:

bonito → **más bonito** → **el más bonito**
nice nicer the nicest

rico → **menos rico**
rich less rich

Este bolso es más bonito que el otro.
This purse is nicer than the other one.

Esta bicicleta es la más cara.
This is the most expensive bicycle.

Some important comparisons are irregular:

bueno good → **mejor** better → **el mejor** the best
malo bad → **peor** worse → **el peor** the worst
grande large → **mayor** larger → **el mayor** the largest
pequeño small → **menor** smaller → **el menor** the smallest
mucho much → **más** more, most
muchos many → **más** more, most
poco little → **menos** less, least
pocos few → **menos** fewer, fewest

There is an absolute superlative, formed by adding **-ísimo;** it is not used in comparisons but has intensive force: **caro** expensive → **carísimo** very expensive; so it is practically equivalent to **muy: muy caro** very expensive.

In the comparison of adverbs, the definite article is **lo: lo más rápidamente posible** the fastest way possible.

Possessive Adjectives

Possessive adjectives agree in number (and the 1st and 2nd person plural also in gender) with the thing possessed, not with the possessor: **su libro** his book, her book, your book, their book; **sus libros** his books, her books, your books, their books.

Singular	Plural
mi, mis my	**nuestro(s), nuestra(s)** our
tu, tus your*	**vuestro(s), vuestra(s)** your*
su, sus your**	**su, sus** your**
su, sus his, her, its	**su, sus** their

*familiar address/**formal address

Stressed froms of possessive adjectives follow the noun they modify and are mainly used in direct address, in exclamations, and as equivalents of English "of mine, of his, of theirs", etc.: **Buenos días, amigo mío.** Good morning, my friend.

Singular	Plural
mío(s), mía(s) my	**nuestro(s), nuestra(s)** our
tuyo(s), tuya(s) your*	**vuestro(s), vuestra(s)** your*
suyo(s), suya(s) your**	**suyo(s), suya(s)** your**
suyo(s), suya(s) his, her, its	**suyo(s), suya(s)** their

*familiar address / **formal address

Demonstrative Adjectives

	este this (near me)		**ese** that (near you)		**aquel** that (yonder)	
	♂	♀	♂	♀	♂	♀
Singular	**este**	**esta**	**ese**	**esa**	**aquel**	**aquella**
Plural	**estos**	**estas**	**esos**	**esas**	**aquellos**	**aquellas**

The neuter "this (here)" is **esto.**

When these forms stand alone without the noun (that is, when they are demonstrative pronouns), the **e** becomes **é: Èste es mi libro.** This is my book. **Quisiera comprar este libro.** I'd like to buy this book. – **¿Cuál, éste?** Which one, this one?

PRONOUNS

Personal Pronouns

	Subject Pronouns		Conjunctive Pronouns Direct object		Indir. object	
sing.	**yo**	I	**me**	me	**me**	to me
	tú	you*	**te**	you*	**te**	to you*
	usted	you**	**le, lo,** *f* **la**	you**	**le**	to you**
	él	he, it	**le**	him	**le**	to him
			lo	him, it		
	ella	she, it	**la**	her	**le**	to her
	ello	it	**lo**	it	**le**	to it
plural	**nosotros, -as**	we	**nos**	us	**nos**	to us
	vosotros, -as	you*	**os**	you*	**os**	to you*
	ustedes	you**	**les, los,** *f* **las**	you**	**les**	to you**
	ellos, -as	they	**los, las**	them	**les, las**	to them

*familiar address / **formal address

Usted (addressing one person) is used with the 3rd person singular. **Ustedes** (addressing several) is used with the 3rd person plural.

The subject pronouns are used for special emphasis. Generally they are omitted; the Spanish verb form is enough to identify the person: **Soy chileno.** I'm from Chile.

Reflexive Pronouns

Singular		Plural	
me	myself, to myself	**nos**	ourselves, to ourselves
te	yourself, to yourself	**os**	yourselves, to yourselves
se	himself, herself itself, to himself, to herself, to itself	**se**	themselves, yourselves, to themselves, to yourselves

Examples: **Él se culpa.** He blames himself. **Me lo pongo.** I put it on. **Se ven en el espejo.** They see themselves/each other in the mirror.

Position of Pronouns

When two conjunctive pronouns are used together, both precede the verb, and the indirect object precedes the direct object: **Te lo compro.** I'm buying it for you.

If two pronouns that are adjacent begin both with an **l,** the first one changes to **se: Se lo regalo.** I give it to her (as a present).

When pronouns are used with an infinitive, they can be placed before the infinitive or appended to the infinitive: **Deseo levantarme temprano.** I wish to get up early. **Quiero comprármelo.** I'd like to buy it (for myself).

VERBS

Present Tense

Spanish has three regular conjugations: verbs ending in **-ar, -er** and **-ir**.

	viajar to travel	comer to eat	vivir to live, to reside
(yo)	viajo	como	vivo
(tú)	viajas	comes	vives
(él/ella/usted)	viaja	come	vive
(nosotros/nosotras)	viajamos	comemos	vivimos
(vosotros/vosotras)	viajáis	coméis	vivís
(ellos/ellas/ustedes)	viajan	comen	viven

In addition, there are the following irregularities:

1. Verbs that **change a vowel**

   The stem of certain verbs changes the vowel in the singular forms and in the 3rd person plural:

e → ie entender to understand	o → ue contar to count, to tell	u → ue jugar to play	e → i pedir to ask for
entiendo	cuento	juego	pido
entiendes	cuentas	juegas	pides
entiende	cuenta	juega	pide
entendemos	contamos	jugamos	pedimos
entendéis	contáis	jugáis	pedís
entienden	cuentan	juegan	piden

2. Verbs that **change a consonant**

   In verbs ending in **-ecer, -ocer,** and **-ucir,** the 1st person singular changes **c** to **zc,** as in **conocer** to (get to) know: **(yo) conozco, (tú) conoces, (él) conoce** etc.

   Some verbs change to a **g** in the 1st person singular, as in **hacer** to make: **(yo) hago, (tú) haces, (él) hace** etc.

3. Verbs with **two changes**

tener to have	decir to say	venir to come	oír to hear
tengo	digo	vengo	oigo
tienes	dices	vienes	oyes
tiene	dice	viene	oye
tenemos	decimos	venimos	oímos
tenéis	decís	venís	oís
tienen	dicen	vienen	oyen

4. Other **irregularities**

   Some of the most important verbs are irregular in the 1st person singular:

   dar to give → **(yo) doy**
   saber to know → **(yo) sé**
   ver to see → **(yo) veo**

5. The verbs **ser, estar** und **ir**

ser to be	**estar** to be	**ir** to go
soy	**estoy**	**voy**
eres	**estás**	**vas**
es	**está**	**va**
somos	**estamos**	**vamos**
sois	**estáis**	**vais**
son	**están**	**van**

For the difference between **ser** and **estar,** see below (page 253).

Past Tenses

The most important past tenses are the preterit, the present perfect, and the imperfect.

The **preterite** ("I traveled") is used with expressions of time such as **ayer** yesterday, **el otro día** the other day, **la semana pasada** last week, or **el año pasado** last year. It is the most common form among the past tenses.

The **present perfect** ("I have traveled") is used only with expressions of time such as **hoy** today, or **esta mañana** this morning.

The **imperfect** ("I was traveling", "I used to travel") refers to an ongoing condition or action in the past:
El hotel era muy barato y teníamos el mar cerca.
The hotel was not expensive, and the ocean was close by.

Preterite

viajar to travel	**comer** to eat	**vivir** to live, to reside
viaj*é*	com*í*	viv*í*
viaj*aste*	com*iste*	viv*iste*
viaj*ó*	com*ió*	viv*ió*
viaj*amos*	com*imos*	viv*imos*
viaj*asteis*	com*isteis*	viv*isteis*
viaj*aron*	com*ieron*	viv*ieron*

The following verbs have a different stem in the preterit:

ser to be	**estar** to be	**hacer** to make
fu*i*	estuv*e*	hic*e*
fu*iste*	estuv*iste*	hic*iste*
fu*e*	estuv*o*	hiz*o*
fu*imos*	estuv*imos*	hic*imos*
fu*isteis*	estuv*isteis*	hic*isteis*
fu*eron*	estuv*ieron*	hic*ieron*

(For the difference between **ser** and **estar,** see below, page 253).

The following verbs have the same endings as **estar:**
decir → **dije** I said
tener → **tuve** I had
poder → **pude** I could
venir → **vine** I came
querer → **quise** I liked

Present perfect

The present perfect is formed with the present tense of **haber** and the past participle. The past participle is formed by adding **-ado** to the stem of verbs ending in **-ar** and by adding **-ido** to the stem of verbs ending in **-er** or **-ir**.

The present forms of **haber** are **he, has, ha; hemos, habéis, han.**

viajar → **he viajado** I have traveled
comer → **he comido** I have eaten
vivir → **he vivido** I have lived, I have resided

Irregular past participles of some important verbs:
abrir → **abierto** opened
escribir → **escrito** written
decir → **dicho** said
hacer → **hecho** made
poner → **puesto** put
ver → **visto** seen
volver → **vuelto** returned

Imperfect

viajar to travel	**comer** to eat	**vivir** to live, to reside
viajaba	comía	vivía
viajabas	comías	vivías
viajaba	comía	vivía
viajábamos	comíamos	vivíamos
viajabais	comíais	vivíais
viajaban	comían	vivían

Nearly all verbs are regular in the imperfect. Exceptions are **ser** and **ir**:

ser to be	**ir** to go
era	iba
eras	ibas
era	iba
éramos	íbamos
erais	ibais
eran	iban

Future Tense

The future tense is formed with the infinitive plus ending. The endings are the same for all three regular conjugations: **-é, -ás, -á, -emos, -éis, -án**; for example, **viajar** → **viajaré** I will travel.

In some irregular verbs the stem changes:
tener → **tendré** I will have
hacer → **haré** I will make
poder → **podré** I will be able to
querer → **querré** I will like
venir → **vendré** I will come
But the endings are the same as for the regular verbs.

It is also customary to express a future action by using the present tense of **ir** + **a** + verb: **Voy a comprar pan.** I'm going to buy bread.

The Conditional

The conditional is formed with the infinitive plus ending. The endings are the same for all three conjugations: **-ía**, **-ías**, **-ía**; **-íamos**, **-íais**, **-ían**; for example, **viajar** → **viajaría** I would travel.

The stem changes found in some irregular verbs are the same as for the future tense (see above).

It is customary to use the conditional as an expression of politeness: **¿Podría ayudarme?** Could you help me?

Ser and estar

In Spanish there are two verbs that mean "to be": **ser** and **estar.** **Ser** expresses mainly a permanent or characteristic state; **estar** expresses mainly a temporary or accidental state; but note these categories:

ser is used for	
origin	**Soy mejicano.** I'm a Mexican.
occupation	**Es mecánico.** He's a mechanic.
relatives	**Es mi padre.** He's my father.
permanent traits	**Juana es alta.** Juana is tall.
	El hierro es duro. Iron is hard.
possession	**Éste es mi libro.** This is my book.
material	**El pantalón es de algodón.** The pants are made of cotton.
BUT ALSO FOR	
time	**Son las cuatro.** It's four o'clock.
	Es tarde. It's late.
day	**Hoy es martes.** Today is Tuesday.

estar is used for	
physical or mental	**Estoy enfermo.** I am sick.
conditions	**Está enfadada.** She is annoyed.
temporary situations	**La puerta está cerrada.** The door is closed.
BUT ALSO FOR	
place names	**Caracas está en Venezuela.** Caracas is in Venezuela.

NEGATIVES

not: **no**
Ésta no es mi maleta. This is not my suitcase.

nothing: **no ... nada**
No entiendo nada. I don't understand anything.

nobody/not ... anybody: **no ... nadie/nadie**
Nadie sabe dónde está mi maleta. Nobody knows where my suitcase ist.
No he visto nadie. I haven't seen anybody.

no more/not ... any more: **ya no ...**
Ya no tenemos gasolina. We have no more gasoline.

never: **no ... nunca/nunca**
No va nunca a comprar. or **Nunca va a comprar.** He/She never goes shopping.

QUESTION WORDS

In interrogative sentences the subject follows the verb:
¿Viene Pepe hoy a cenar? Is Pepe coming for dinner today?

The most important question words:

how?	**¿cómo?**	**¿Cómo está?** How are you?
how much?	**¿cuánto?**	**¿Cuánto cuesta?** How much does it cost?

what?	**¿qué?**	**¿Qué ha dicho?** What did you say?
when?	**¿cuándo?**	**¿Cuándo se van del hotel?** When will you leave the hotel?
where?	**¿dónde?**	**¿Dónde está la parada del bus?** Where is the bus stop?
where to?	**¿adónde?**	**¿Adónde va este tren?** Where does this train go (to)?
which?	**¿cuál?**	**¿Cuál es el camino más corte?** Which is the shortest way?
who?	**¿quién?**	**¿Quién es el responsable del hotel?** Who is in charge of the hotel?
whom?	**¿a quién?**	**¿A quién tengo que llamar?** Whom do I have to call?
to whom?	**¿a quién?**	**¿A quién le has dado las llaves?** (To) whom did you give the keys?
whose?	**¿de quién?**	**¿De quién es el coche?** Whose car is it?
why?	**¿por qué?**	**¿Por qué no va usted en taxi?** Why don't you take a taxi?

Some of the question words take plural or gender endings: **¿quién? → ¿quiénes? / ¿cuál? → ¿cuáles? / cuànto? → ¿cuántos, -a, -as?**

NUMBERS

Cardinal Numbers

0 **cero** se'rō
1 **uno** o͞o'nō
2 **dos** dōs
3 **tres** tres
4 **cuatro** ko͞o·ä'trō
5 **cinco** sēng'kō
6 **seis** se'ēs
7 **siete** sye'te
8 **ocho** ō'tshō
9 **nueve** no͞o·e've
10 **diez** dyes'
11 **once** ōn'se
12 **doce** dō'se
13 **trece** tre'se
14 **catorce** kätōr'se
15 **quince** kēn'se
16 **dieciséis** dyesēse'ēs
17 **diecisiete** dyesēsye'te
18 **dieciocho** dyesē·ō'tshō
19 **diecinueve** dyesēno͞o·e've
20 **veinte** ve'ēnte
21 **veintiuno** ve·ēntē·o͞o'nō
22 **veintidós** ve·ēntē·dōs'
23 **veintitrés** ve·ēntētres'
24 **veinticuatro** ve·ēntēko͞o·ä'trō

25 **veinticinco** ve·ēntēsēng'kō
26 **veintiséis** ve·ēntēse'ēs
27 **veintisiete** ve·ēntēsye'te
28 **veintiocho** ve·ēntē·ō'tshō
29 **veintinueve** ve·ēntēnōō·e've
30 **treinta** tre'ēntä
40 **cuarenta** kōō·ären'tä
50 **cincuenta** sēng·kōō·en'tä
60 **sesenta** sesen'tä
70 **setenta** seten'tä
80 **ochenta** ōtshen'tä
90 **noventa** nōven'tä
100 **cien** syen'
101 **ciento uno** syen'tō ōō'nō
200 **doscientos** dōsyen'tōs
1000 **mil** mēl
2000 **dos mil** dōs mēl
10000 **diez mil** dyes' mēl

Ordinal Numbers

1. **primero** prēme'rō
2. **segundo** segōōn'dō
3. **tercero** terse'rō
4. **cuarto** kōō·är'tō
5. **quinto** kēn'tō
6. **sexto** seks'tō
7. **séptimo** sep'tēmō
8. **octavo** ōktä'vō
9. **noveno** nōve'nō